Saint Thérèse of Lisieux and her Sisters

JENNIFER MOORCROFT

GRACEWING

First published in 2014 by
Gracewing
2 Southern Avenue
Leominster
Herefordshire HR6 0QF
United Kingdom
www.gracewing.co.uk

ISBN 978 085244 846 5

Typeset by Gracewing

Cover design by Bernardita Peña Hurtado

Contents

INTRODUCTION

I HAVE A BOOK on drawing which advocates a method by which, rather than concentrating on the object, one draws the outline and then the object takes shape. This is the approach I have taken in this book.

So much has been written about Saint Thérèse of Lisieux that it is almost invidious to think that more can be explored. Instead, I was interested in those around her who would describe themselves as 'lesser souls' compared to Thérèse, but who nevertheless put into practice her 'Little Way', those who were part of her life, both in her family and in the monastery. In biographies of Thérèse they appear almost like bit-players in her life, in the periphery, a background to the canvas on which she is painted. But these people are interesting in their own right, so varied in their personalities; ones who were touched by Thérèse and whose lives were changed by her, but who also played a part in forming her in becoming the saint she was.

Like one of her novices, Sister Martha, I have always felt somewhat daunted by Thérèse, something that might surprise since she described herself as a little soul. But she lived what she described as her 'Little Way' to such perfection and with such a single minded purpose that it could be off-putting to lesser souls, just as it was to Martha. However, the example of those around her could be helpful in showing the various ways in which her spiritual teaching could be lived out.

Thérèse has been described as the greatest saint of modern times, opening up to all her little way of love and surrender. She can be viewed as unique but in fact her message was nothing new, for it was part of the Church's spiritual patrimony; and, as Thérèse herself discovered, it was imbedded deep in Scripture, both in the Old Testament and in the New. Every saint and every Christian is called to live in loving surrender to God's will, which is the essence of the Little Way.

However, she lived at a time that had been infected by Jansenism, a rigid spirituality with an emphasis on the justice of God and an emphasis on 'doing' things for God. Even in her family there was a trace of Jansenism, although it was sweetened there by the dominating sense of the love of the good God. As a child Thérèse was encouraged to keep a record of her virtues and sacrifices and in the Lisieux Carmel there was more importance attached to mortifications offered up to appease the justice of God than on the love of God. Her 'Little Way', then, was truly revolutionary in bringing back to the Gospel of God's love souls brought up in that atmosphere.

When talking about her 'sisters', this covers various groups. First of all are the two elder sisters, Marie and Pauline, who, after the death of their mother brought up Thérèse and formed her in the Christian life, but who in turn became her disciples. Another elder sister, Léonie, was the only sister not to enter the Lisieux Carmel, instead becoming, after many vicissitudes, a Visitation sister; she was, perhaps more than any other, a true saint of the Little Way. Céline straddles both groups, being both Thérèse's sister and also her novice after her entry into Carmel.

In Carmel, Thérèse was given the care of five novices, and was able to pass on her teaching and shape it in many different ways that best suited the very disparate group of young women under her care.

I explore those sisters who were both her fellow novices and who were also under her direction. Then, there were other sisters in the Carmel, those who were responsible for her training, such as the redoubtable Mother Marie de Gonzague and the gentle Mother Marie of the Angels, her Novice Mistress. There were those sisters in the community who, by their unkindness, forged in her a robust understanding of what it was to truly love others with the love of God himself. Each one was a unique person, each one profoundly influenced by Thérèse. I want to bring them out of the shadows and see how each one, in their different ways and to what extent, lived out the 'Little Way'.

I wish to express my thanks to Fr James McCaffrey ODC and Joanne Mosley of the 'Mount Carmel' magazine for their unfailing encouragement. The chapters on Céline, Léonie, Marie of the Trinity and Marie of the Eucharist are expanded from articles I have written for the magazine over the years, and are used in that sense with Fr McCaffrey's permission.

1

SISTER MARIE OF THE SACRED HEART

MARIE MARTIN

OF THE FOUR Martin sisters Marie, the eldest, seems to be the one least well- known. Pauline is famous as Mother Agnès, who was Thérèse's Prioress for a while. Céline was her childhood companion and one of her novices. Even Léonie, 'poor Léonie', who was such a problem for her family, has had a book written about her. Marie seems to be always in the background, and yet she had a vital role to play in Thérèse's life.

Marie was born in Alençon 22 February 1860, of Louis and Azélie (affectionately known as Zélie) Martin. Both Louis and Zélie had wanted to enter the religious life but had (providentially) been rejected, so Louis became a watchmaker and Zélie set up her own business as a lacemaker. An encounter on a bridge, when Zélie heard interiorly the words, 'This is he whom I have been preparing for you', brought them together, and they were married 13 July 1858 in the church of Notre-Dame in Alençon. At the beginning of their married life it seemed as if they would not have children, since they had decided to live as brother and sister, until a priest showed them the deficiency of this in a married couple.

Having accepted the advice of the wise priest, it was not long before Zélie became pregnant; but during the pregnancy she became ill. She now longed for a child, and was terrified lest the illness would affect her unborn child. Happily, a daughter was born 22 February 1860 and baptised the following day, given the name Marie Louise - all the subsequent daughters received the first name of Marie, in honour of Our Lady, but, apart from Marie herself, were always known by their second name. At her baptism Louis, the proud father, said to the priest, 'It is the first time that you have seen me here for a baptism, but it will not be the last'.

Despite Zélie's fears, Marie was a strong and healthy child, and was followed the next year by a little sister, Pauline. The two girls began their education at home under the watchful eye of their mother, who was concerned to bring them up with a strong Christian ethos. Following the custom of the time, she encouraged them to make little sacrifices, which were seen as jewels or gifts offered to Jesus, with a reward that he would store up for them in heaven. Marie told of an occasion when she was four years old and her mother asked her to give up a cherished basket to Pauline. Zélie encouraged her with the thought that it would put an extra pearl in her heavenly crown. 'I ran quickly to Mama and said, "I've given Pauline the basket; will I go to heaven now?"' Marie related. 'Yes, my daughter, you will go to heaven.' This hope was enough to console Marie for the loss of her toy.

Their father gave nicknames to his girls; Marie was aptly named 'Diamond', which suited her bright and somewhat sharp character. In her family Marie was known as the 'Bohemian' and Ida Gorrës describes her as of a

> forceful and simple nature. Earthy and straightforward, natural and a little angular, with a refreshing love of liberty and a pleasant portion of obstinacy, she was of the stuff out of which—in the next generation—eccentric, professionally active spinsters were made.[1]

When Marie was eight her parents decided to send her and Pauline as boarders to the Visitation school at Le Mans where Mme Martin's sister, Elise, was a nun, Sister Marie- Dosithée. Mme Martin wrote to her sister that, 'Marie appears to be reserved and shy; underneath her shyness is a heart of gold.' Marie-Dosithée had a great influence on the Martin sisters, imbuing them with the gentle and commonsense spirituality of Saint Francis de Sales. Both girls were excellent scholars, although their time at Le Mans was interrupted by various traumatic events.

On 19 July 1870, the Franco-Prussian War began. France declared war on Prussia, but the French soon realised that the German Federation was far stronger. The northern French cities began to fall under the Prussian advance and Louis Martin travelled the dangerous roads to Le Mans to bring his daughters back to Alençon. That town, too, fell to the Germans, and the family were forced to billet nine soldiers in their house until the war ended on 10 May 1871. The girls were then able to return to Le Mans and their schooling.

Soon after the war ended, the Martins inherited a larger property from Mme Martin's father on the rue Saint-Blaise and the family moved into it; this gave room for Zélie to expand her lace-making business. It came at a providential time, because Louis had incurred substantial losses in their stock holdings, due to the collapse of the French economy as a result of the war. Louis sold up his watchmaking business so that he could take over the business side of Zélie's lacemaking.

There were family tragedies, too; of the nine children born to Zélie, only five survived. Two longed-for boys and two girls died in their infancy or soon after birth. Of these, only Hélène, a delightful child, survived beyond her fourth birthday. Zélie was a tireless worker, and with the demands of her lacemaking and the gradual onset of the breast cancer that eventually killed her, she was unable to breastfeed the children herself. She was therefore forced to put the babies out to wet-nurses, something that was fairly common at the time, but which was to have disastrous consequences. Both their boys died of gastro-enteritis, which was not uncommon due to the water pollution in the badly maintained sewage systems of the time.

When Zélie's eighth child, Marie-Mélanie-Thérèse, was born in 1870, she reluctantly placed the child with a wet-nurse on the rue du Barre nearby to be cared for. She had seemed an excellent choice, she was clean, and the house well kept, but Marie proved to be very perceptive and later said that the wet-nurse 'did not have an honest look'. She was ten years old at the time, and at home because of the war. She went one day with the family's maid, Louise, to visit her little sister. When they arrived, the woman immediately put little Marie-Mélanie to her breast as if to prove her industriousness, but Marie noticed that the baby fell on it as if she was starving. Marie said as much to Louise on the way home, but the servant dismissed her worries out of hand. It preyed on Marie's mind so much, though, that eventually, looking at some bread she remarked to her mother, 'Ah, if little Thérèse had just a morsel of that, she wouldn't be dying of hunger'. Her alarmed mother at once demanded to know the truth and went immediately to take back her baby. Alas, it was too late to save her, and her death weighed heavily on Marie. She had noticed that her mother never cried over the loss of her children—her loss went too deep even for tears—but that her mother was strengthened by the conviction that the little ones were now in heaven; it was this thought that consoled and reassured Marie, too. Zélie, though, found it almost too unbearable to go past the cemetery where her little ones were buried.

When she was thirteen years old Marie contracted typhoid and had to be sent home while Pauline stayed at the school alone over the Easter holidays. Both her parents were distraught, because typhoid at that time could be fatal. Her father made a pilgrimage to pray for her recovery, she soon turned the corner, and on the feast of the Ascension she was able to go outside for the first time. At her confirmation shortly afterwards Marie took the name of Josephine in thanksgiving to St Joseph's intercession in helping her recovery.

When Marie completed her schooling in 1875, she returned home to take over the running of the household. However well she did at school, leaving with several of the top honours, Marie herself seemed to have had a less favourable impression of her school years, remarking, 'Oh, if I had not had my aunt, whom I did not want to hurt, I should have never remained seven years behind those grilles'. She was certainly not enamoured with religious life.

Her mother had a high regard for her eldest daughter, writing to Sister Marie-Dosithée, 'Marie is now grown up; her character is of a very serious cast and she has none of the illusions of youth. I am sure that when I am no longer here she will make a good mistress of the home, and do her utmost to bring up her little sisters and set a good example.'

Zélie needed to have that assurance, because the breast cancer was progressing rapidly. She was anxious, too, to see her eldest daughter settle down with a family of her own, but when her mother broached the idea of marriage Marie was firm in her response, saying that she would never marry; she begged her mother not to bring the subject up again. Seeing the heartbreak of her mother losing so many of her children could have been a big contributory factor to her aversion to married life. Instead, she devoted herself to looking after the family she did have. Zélie's last child, Thérèse, had been born 2 January 1873, and Marie was proud and delighted to be named as her godmother when she was baptised two days later. It was a role that mattered a great deal to both of them.

Marie had a good business head and also took over the book-keeping side of her mother's lace-making business: 'Louise, who has just come in, was saying: "This room is soon going to be like a notary's office,"'[2] she wrote to Pauline, who was still at school, describing her room in the family home. In addition, she was giving lessons to the three younger children, Léonie, Céline and Thérèse. Thérèse was four years old by then, but insisted on sharing Céline's lessons; she was already able to understand some of it. Zélie's greatest concern was that the girls would be brought up to have a strong faith, and she was content to see that Marie was more than competent in this.

Zélie died at dawn 28 August 1877, and a few days later, as the five girls were sadly huddled together after the funeral, Louise said to them, with a deal of tactlessness, 'Poor little things, you have no mother any more'. Thérèse recounts how Céline threw her arms around Marie, crying, 'Well, you will be my Mamma now', and Thérèse, not to be outdone, ran into Marie's arms, crying, 'Well as for me, it's Pauline will be my Mamma'.[3]

Marie took over her role as mother to all the young children. Pauline had left school by this time and in her turn helped Marie to bring up their three youngest sisters. Their uncle, Zélie's brother, Isidore Guérin, suggested that the family sell their house in Alençon and move to be near them in Lisieux, where the Guérins became almost their second family; indeed, Isidore referred to the five Martin sisters as their adopted daughters. They found a beautiful house which they named La Buissonets, and which became their much-loved family home.

Pauline had long been considering her religious vocation, and on 2 October 1882 she entered the Lisieux Carmel. This was a terrible blow to Thérèse and, following on from the loss of her mother, triggered the illness that almost killed her, and from which she was cured by the vision of 'Our Lady of the Smile'. It was Marie who nursed and cared for her during this fraught and worrying time, Marie who knelt by her bedside praying for a cure. As Thérèse herself wrote: 'And so, in reality, I had only Marie, and she was indispensable to me, so to speak… I loved her so much I couldn't live without her.'[4] Thérèse was suffering from scruples at the time, and she confessed each smallest peccadillo to Marie, who 'weeded them out' so that she confessed only a certain amount to her confessor.

Marie also prepared the younger girls for their First Holy Communion; Thérèse recalled vividly the preparations she made with the help of both Pauline (now Sister Agnès of Jesus), and Marie. In the manner of the time she kept a tally of her sacrifices and her offerings of love to Jesus on a little chaplet. However, this tutoring didn't always go smoothly. Marie could be sharp-tongued and the young ones sometimes rebelled against her instruction, their religious as well as their school lessons. Léonie stubbornly refused to keep the list of her little sacrifices and 'offerings', and although Marie said that Thérèse was never disobedient, a childhood friend, Marguérite-Marie, disagreed and said that she had to advise Thérèse to be more submissive to her. Thérèse herself confessed to Mother Marie de Gonzague that she was always answering her sister back when she told her to do something.

It might have seemed that Marie's vocation was to continue looking after the family, including her father, and so it was a great shock when Marie declared that she, too, wanted to enter the Lisieux Carmel. Her father was devastated, because he thought she would always be there to look after him. She spoke to him of her vocation in April/May of 1886, and Marie recalled how 'he sighed at such a revelation! He was far from expecting it, for nothing in me could have made him suspect that I wanted to be a religious.' The Guérins, too, were astounded, because, as Marie recalled, 'They did not want to believe me; they were absolutely stunned. I, the independent one! I, who never seemed to be able to stand convents, and I was about to become a religious? They could not get over their surprise.'[5]

It seemed that this call to the cloister was one more of pragmatism than the burning desire that had drawn

Pauline, and that it was mostly at the urging of her confessor, the Jesuit priest, Fr Almire Pichon. He had come to Lisieux in April 1882 to preach a retreat which Marie attended, and after Mass she stepped into the confessional saying in her blunt and forthright manner, 'Father, I only came to see a saint'. It seems that she had found what she was looking for.

Marie was now twenty-two and did want to become a nun, but not necessarily a cloistered, contemplative one. She was also waiting for a sign from God as to what he wanted for her. In the confessional she spoke to Fr Pichon of her desire to be a nun and also her reservations. He advised her to write down her thoughts, and she covered eight pages, which she discussed with him. After this discussion, Marie felt as if she had been caught in 'the nets of divine mercy' and now knew what she had to do. Fr Pichon became her spiritual director 17 April 1882, and on 25 March 1885 she made a vow of chastity. As for Fr Pichon, he looked forward to the day when his 'fiery child would become a lamb'.

He became not only Marie's spiritual director but also a close and well loved family friend. He was well able to guide the Martin family, because, like Thérèse he had suffered severely from scruples. He was cured of them only when he entered the Jesuits; there, he was guided into an attitude of simplicity and trust, which was far from the rigid Jansenism that affected French Catholicism of the time and even to a certain extent, the Martin family, with its insistence on counting their virtues and acts. To Almire Pichon, the Sacred Heart was the wondrous symbol of that overwhelming love of God for his children, and he became a noted apostle of the Sacred Heart devotion.

Marie visited her sister Pauline in Carmel every week and found, in her own words, that 'I used to return to Carmel as to the spring of all my happiness.' What she did not realise, though, was that these visits, when she also took Céline and Thérèse, was a source of immense anguish for Thérèse. Marie and Pauline were engrossed with talking to each other, and the younger girls had only a few minutes at the end of the visit to speak with Pauline themselves. Thérèse, ultra sensitive and longing to speak to the sister who was such a mother to her, invariably ended the visit in tears.

Pauline, now Sister Agnès, was urging Marie to enter the Carmel as soon as possible. She pointed out that Céline was now old enough to take over the running of the household, and began a spirited correspondence on the subject. 'If you only knew how much I long for you, how I sense more and more that your place is here, beside me in this little, blessed cloister,' she wrote to her. 'Mother Geneviève told me that she does nothing but think of you. She is a saint whose prayers can do great things.' 'I will enter when the good God tells me to,' retorted Marie, 'but he hasn't shown his will clearly.' 'I don't believe he'll show you in this way,' replied Agnès. 'You are coming up to twenty six years of age. It is time to make a decision.' 'I will not do this for myself,' was her sister's response. 'Since he well knows that I want only to do his will, perhaps he will send me an angel to tell me.'

On 15 August, Marie received a decisive confirmation from Fr Pichon: 'After having prayed very much, I believe I am the interpreter of Our Lord, giving you the signal of departure, of going out of Egypt. Go quickly with a joyful heart to hide in His Heart.'[6]

However much Marie saw the Lisieux Carmel as the spring of all her happiness, which was, perhaps, what she felt in hindsight, she was at the time still ambivalent. Although she said she was caught in the nets of divine mercy and it was a gentle and persistent call, they were nets nevertheless. 'I have found God's mercy too bitter at times, but we must nevertheless respond to it no matter how hard it may be,' she wrote to the Guérins.[7]

She entered Lisieux Carmel 15 October 1886, and in a letter he wrote to her that day, her uncle acknowledged that her entry had none of the sweetness it had had for Pauline:

> The sacrifice, then, is complete, and what a sacrifice: your youth, your beauty, family, tastes, well-being, freedom and the world!... For Pauline, He casts roses beneath her feet; she is pierced by the thorns, but the scent of the roses inebriates her and the Beloved's melodious voice lessens the suffering. From you, my dear, He hides the roses; the thorns alone strike your view, and He is spreading them abundantly beneath your feet.[8]

Marie took the name of Marie of the Sacred Heart, perhaps in gratitude to Fr Pichon's devotion, and as a postulant was dressed in a long blue dress with a black mantle over it and a black lace bonnet on her head. One of her tasks was sweeping and other household tasks for which she needed another bonnet, and rather than wear her night cap, the other alternative, she asked Céline and Thérèse to find something suitable. The only one they found was a rather stylish one from Mme Caval's shop in town and Marie wrote back to them:

> Sister Marie of the Sacred Heart prefers her night cap to this piece of vanity. I'm sorry for having given you this trouble uselessly. You should return this bonnet and get something else. When Thérèse comes, Our Mother [Mother Marie de Gonzague] said this evening *she herself* will make her little bonnets.[9]

The sacrifice was no less for those she left behind. It was left to the seventeen year old Céline to take over the running of the house, and she felt the loss of Marie keenly. She had chosen Marie to be her second mother after their mother's death, and now: 'I am all alone in life,' she wrote to Mother Marie de Gonzague. 'I am deprived of my dear Marie, whom I love so much! I cannot resign myself to this thought; it seems to me it is something unreal, and yet, it is only too true.'[10] The time was even more fraught because, only a week before Marie's entry, Léonie had suddenly entered the Poor Clares in her first, abortive attempt to enter the religious life. Thérèse was also distraught at losing yet another 'mother'; her loneliness increased, but it also deepened her own calling to Carmel.

She had already confided this desire to Marie, something that Marie touched on in her reference to the Prioress making her bonnets, but when this began to take definite shape Marie was one of those who were adamantly against it. She considered that Thérèse was too young and immature, and she was afraid that it would cause their father even greater grief because of the special place Thérèse held in his life, 'the true sunshine of his life'. It was also a relatively short time since she had put Thérèse on her knee to prepare her for her Holy Communion, and seeing her little sister so often in tears and knowing her keen sensitivity, she perhaps felt that she did not have the spiritual robustness for the austerity of Carmelite life. She had not been at Les Buissonets for the Christmas of 1886, when Thérèse received her 'grace of conversion', and did not know of the immense strides her sister was making in her spiritual life and in her maturity. She accepted that Thérèse did indeed have a vocation, but just not yet. She wrote to Thérèse, reminding her of what the Pope had said to her during her audience in Rome, that she would enter when God willed it, and encouraged her young sister to accept God's will.

Marie was clothed with the habit on the Feast of St Joseph 1887, a saint very dear to her, and was therefore still a novice herself when Thérèse entered the Carmel the following year, 9 April 1888. Marie was made her 'angel', the sister who would introduce her to the customs and practices of Carmel, and if indeed she had doubts about her youngest sister's maturity, these doubts were soon laid to rest. Although austere in many ways, Mother Marie de Gonzague allowed great laxity in other areas, including the rule of silence. She assumed that this time of proximity would allow the two sisters to speak freely with each other, but right from the very beginning Thérèse was determined to keep the Rule in its fullness and refused to accept this little bit of comfort. Marie wrote later:

> From the very first days of her novitiate, I saw the degree to which she would be faithful to the Rule. It was hardly three weeks that she was in Carmel, and thinking that she did not know how to find the [Divine] Office alone, I wanted to keep her with me to teach her how to find the commemorations. But instead of taking advantage of this opportunity [to be alone with Marie

> and speak to her] she answered sweetly: 'I thank you, I found them today. I would be happy to stay with you, but it is better that I deprive myself, for we are not at home!'[11]

Marie made her Profession 22 May 1888 and received the black veil the following day; Thérèse crowned her with the traditional roses and Fr Pichon preached the sermon; he stayed for several more days to give retreat sermons to the community, because it was also the 50th anniversary of the founding of the Carmel.

Although this was a time of rejoicing, bad news arrived, too. Her father had attended the ceremony of Marie's taking of the veil, and began showering the monastery with gifts. This was somewhat of a mixed blessing, because some of the Community resented the fact that this largesse came from the Martin family. Thérèse was often given the task of thanking her father for them, but did it very discreetly. Then in June, Céline approached her father about her own religious vocation, which seems to have been the trigger for a deterioration in his health. He suddenly disappeared for several days and was eventually found in Le Havre, and for the next four years, as his health deteriorated more and more, gave all his daughters increasing anguish until his death 29 July 1894.

As Marie was approaching the end of her time in the Novitiate she was made second infirmarian and helped nurse the saintly founder of the Carmel, Mother Geneviève of St Teresa, and was able to benefit from her example. She gained such an appreciation of the elderly nun's holiness that after Thérèse's death she replied to a visiting priest, Mgr Picaud, in the parlour, who asked her if Mother Geneviève was a saint, 'A much greater saint than Thérèse!' Marie was no friend of suffering, and her fear of suffering might have been compounded by witnessing at first hand the appalling sufferings that Mother Geneviève endured over several years.

She was also the recipient of her wisdom and insight. One day, she was grieving over having to miss her prayer time; Mother Geneviève discerned this and said to her, 'My child, do you know what Our Lord has just revealed to me? These are His own words: 'It is not the souls who spend all their time praying who are most pleasing to me, but those who prove their love by sacrifice and obedience.'[12]

Another time Marie saw Mother Marie de Gonzague talking to some sisters and was tempted to stop and listen, but resisted the temptation and walked on. Arriving at the infirmary, Mother Geneviève said to her, 'I have a little secret to tell you, my child—how to be always happy and to please Our Lord. Never try to find out what is going on. If you see Reverend Mother talking to some of the sisters, instead of stopping, make a sacrifice of your curiosity to God'. Marie was astonished at this because the invalid could not possibly have seen her. 'I did not see you,' Mother Geneviève replied with her sweet smile, 'but Our Lord, no doubt, allows me to tell you this for your good.'[13]

Marie left the Novitiate 5 July 1891, and took her place as a full Chapter sister in the community. Three years later she was given the post of bursar, in charge of the community's finances, a post she held until 1933, when her health had deteriorated too far to enable her to continue.

Marie had less contact with Thérèse once she had left the Novitiate but retained a deep respect for her, seeing in her a depth of spirituality that surpassed hers. Writing to her father shortly after she left the Novitiate and thanking him for his gifts to the community, she referred to the nicknames that her father had given them: Diamond, Pearl, and for Thérèse, Queen, adding, 'your Queen is really worthy of this title; she is a little Queen, a perfection worthy of her King.'[14]

Even she, though, did not comprehend the depths of charity and love that were propelling Thérèse so rapidly along the path of holiness. She could not help noticing that Thérèse was showing a particular liking for another sister who had such an awkward character that most of the sisters avoided her as much as possible. Unknown to Marie—and to that sister, too—Thérèse also had a great aversion to her, but hid it so well that Marie thought she loved the sister very much. 'I felt jealous. One day I said to her: "I cannot help telling you in confidence about something that is annoying me … I think you love Sister—more than me, and I don't think it's fair. After all, God made family ties. You always seem so pleased to see her that I cannot think otherwise, since you have never shown such happiness about being with me." She laughed heartily at this, but she gave me no idea of the aversion she felt for this religious.'[15]

It is understandable that Marie should feel hurt, with her god-daughter seemingly preferring someone else to her, especially as family ties were so strong between the Martin sisters. Thérèse, though, was living her religious life in all its rigour, in a new family; above all she was extending her love beyond her family to express her limitless love in the practical trials of everyday life within her community, a love that reached out to embrace the whole world. At this time Marie did not understand this. Nevertheless, Thérèse still loved her family with an intense and tender love, as the many letters and notes between them testify. She still remembered her family life with great affection, and it was when she was recounting some stories of her early life during recreation during the winter of 1894 that Marie had an inspiration that would galvanise the world. As she explained it in her own words:

One winter's evening after Matins, Sister Thérèse, Sister Genevieve [Céline, who had entered earlier that year], Mother Agnès of Jesus, then Prioress [Pauline, who had been elected Prioress the previous year], and I, were warming ourselves together. Sister Thérèse related two or three incidents from her childhood. I said to Mother Agnès: 'Is it possible that you should permit her to compose little poems to please everybody, and that she should not write anything about all the memories of her childhood? You'll see yet that she is an angel who will not remain long on earth, and we shall have lost all these detailed accounts that we find so interesting'. Mother Prioress hesitated at first; then, at our insistence, she told the Servant of God that it would give her much pleasure if she would give her an account of her childhood for her feastday.[16]

Thérèse duly wrote the account, which she gave to Mother Agnès over a year later, on 20 January 1896, for her feast day the following day. Mother Agnès put it to one side for lack of time and did not read it until she ceased being Prioress later that year. Marie herself did not read it until the following year, when Thérèse was terminally ill. This became Manuscript A in the book that was later published as 'Story of a Soul'.

On Trinity Sunday 9 June 1895, Thérèse made her Act of Oblation, and two days later Céline made it with her. Thérèse also wanted Marie to make it and while they were haymaking in the meadow later in the year, she came up her sister and spoke of it to her. 'Certainly not,' replied Marie. 'I am not going to offer myself as a victim; God would take me at my word, and suffering frightens me too much.'

Thérèse answered that she understood, but that to offer oneself as a victim to God's love was not at all the same thing as offering oneself to his justice; that I would not suffer more; that it was in order to be able to love God better for those who do not want to love him. Thérèse spoke so eloquently that she won Marie over, and Marie never regretted it.[17]

Marie's reluctance to make the Act of Oblation must be seen in the light of the practice common in the Carmels of the time, for religious to offer themselves up as victims to God's justice, averting God's wrath, as they saw it, from sinners on to themselves. It was Thérèse's genius that she turned this practice on its head and invited others to follow her in offering themselves rather as victims to the love of God, to be invaded and transformed by that love and thus be a channel of love to be poured out for others. Like Mother Agnès, Marie had no idea of the depth of Thérèse's union with God until she read the account of her young sister's early life, and wanted to know more. They spoke together about the subject, and when Thérèse went into what would be her last retreat beginning 8 September, Our Lady's Birthday, she received permission to write to Marie, giving her more understanding of what she meant. These letters became Manuscript B in *Story of a Soul*.

To Marie, Thérèse was 'his privileged little spouse', dearly loved of God. 'Ask Jesus to love me, too, as He does His little Thérèse', she wrote to her. Marie was afraid of God's love and the demands it might make on her, yet at the same time she longed to love Jesus with the love she saw so profoundly in Thérèse, and to know and experience his love for herself:

> I ask her to pray very much for her little godmother who loves her so much so that she, too, closing her eyes on all things of the earth, may no longer dream of anything but of looking up above, of working for heaven, of exercising herself in the art of loving. This is the precious pearl that little Thérèse possesses. Little godmother would really like to enjoy this treasure with her.[18]

Thérèse wrote back a long letter, sending with it the sublime pages of Manuscript B. Marie was stunned and read the pages with a mixture of joy and sadness: 'My joy, when I see to what a degree you are loved and privileged; for my sorrow, when I have a foreboding of the desire that Jesus has to pluck His little flower!'

She had long had this foreboding. At the time of Thérèse's First Communion, Thérèse had asked Marie permission to make a half hour of prayer each day. She refused, and even refused a quarter hour of prayer. This refusal sprung from fear: 'I found her so devout, and possessed of such an understanding of supernatural things that it made me afraid, so to speak; my fear was that God would take her to himself too soon.'[19] She repeated that fear when she asked Thérèse to write down her childhood recollections, and now this fear was being realised.

She was afraid, too, of Thérèse's longing for martyrdom. 'Martyrdom was the dream of my youth and this dream has grown within me within Carmel's cloisters,' Thérèse wrote to her. 'But here again, I felt that my dream is a folly, for I cannot confine myself to desiring one kind of martyrdom. To satisfy me I need all.'[20] Marie responded that this desire was not for her:

> Like the young man in the Gospel, a certain feeling of sadness came over me in view of your extraordinary desire for martyrdom. That is the proof of your love; yes, you possess love, but I myself! No, never will you make me believe that I can attain this desired goal, for I dread all that you love.'[21]

It is a reaction that all but a few exceptional souls would have, and Thérèse acknowledges that it is a desire that God himself had put into her soul and not something she would glory in as setting her apart. All she possessed was her poverty. Further, she will not accept that her sister doesn't possess the love and generosity of spirit to embrace whatever was God's will for her:

> Are you not ready to suffer all that God will desire? I really know that you are ready; therefore, if you want to feel joy, to have an attraction for suffering, it is your consolation that you are seeking, since when we love a thing the pain disappears. I assure you, if we were to go to martyrdom together in the dispositions we are in now, you would have great merit, and I would have none at all, unless Jesus was pleased to change my dispositions.[22]

Marie longed to have the love that Thérèse possessed but felt herself so far behind her little sister, who, she was convinced, was possessed by Jesus:

> I wanted to cry when I read these lines that are not from earth but an echo from the Heart of

> God … Do you want me to tell you? Well, you are possessed by God, but what is called … absolutely possessed, just as the wicked are possessed by the devil. I would like to be possessed, too, by good Jesus. However, I love you so much that I rejoice when seeing you are more privileged than I am.[23]

There was a third piece of writing that Marie inspired, and that was a long poem to Our Lady that Thérèse wrote for her during May 1897. From her very earliest years Thérèse had had a deep love of Our Lady and one of her longings to be a priest was so that she could preach a proper sermon on her. She felt that many priests lauded Mary so much that she was taken out of the sphere of an ordinary Christian; Thérèse wanted to focus on the ordinariness of her life, and in her poem traced Mary's life from the Annunciation to her Assumption into heaven. Thérèse said that to her Mary was more mother than Queen, but nevertheless she frequently addresses her as Queen in the poem. Thérèse could have overreached herself in emphasising the ordinary life Mary lived, but with her unerring spiritual sense she did not do so. It is a beautifully balanced meditation that ponders Mary's uniqueness within the bounds of a humdrum life.

Marie could only look on helplessly as Thérèse's health declined, she, who had so longed, and felt sure, that her sister would not suffer. However, she herself was the cause of some suffering for her young sister. Until her twenty-first birthday Thérèse was exempt from the fast, but throughout her time in the monastery, because she was young, seemingly robust and uncomplaining, the sisters in the kitchen often gave her the leftovers. When she became ill, Marie, who had various 'offices' within the monastery—assistant infirmarian, gardener and refectorian, for example, besides her post as bursar - was at the time the Provisor in the kitchen, overseeing the meals and the menu, and so was in a position to help Thérèse by sometimes giving her more nourishing and pleasant food to help her. But, as Thérèse recalled, 'God saw to it that her taste and mine are completely opposed, and that I never had to overcome myself so much as during this period even though I seemed to others thoroughly pampered.'[24]

When Thérèse was finally taken to the infirmary 8 July, Mother Marie de Gonzague gave the Martin sisters permission to be with her as often as they wished. Céline was made assistant to the infirmarian, so was almost constantly with her sister; Mother Agnès, too, no longer Prioress, was able to be with her frequently. Agnès began to record in as much detail as she could Thérèse's 'Last Conversations'. Marie's duties meant that she was able to spend less time with her sister, and recorded much less of what her sister said to her. Nevertheless, she could squeeze in times to be with her. Thérèse knew that Marie was still disturbed and upset over some of the sisters in the community, and advised her to 'rise above everything the Sisters may say, everything they may do. You must act as though you were not in your monastery, as though you had to spend only two days here. You must take care not to say what displeases you, since you must leave it.'

Thérèse had another piece of advice to give her; the bell for the *Salve Regina* was ringing, but Marie continued writing down what Thérèse had said. Thérèse then added, 'It would have been better, far better, to lose those words and go and perform a community act. If we only realized what this means!'[25] She wanted Marie to see that the smallest act of obedience could be an act of love for God.

Earlier on, Marie might have thought Thérèse preferred another sister to her, but she was in no doubt now about the depth of the love her young sister had for her. 'I wanted a word from her,' Marie recalled, 'such as whether she remembered the past and the devotedness with which I surrounded her in her childhood. Scarcely had the thought come, when she raised eyes filled with tears to Mother Agnès of Jesus and myself, and said, "Little sisters … it's you who raised me!"'[26]

As Marie looked at her tenderly a few days later Thérèse said to her, 'Godmother, how beautiful you look when your face is lit up with a ray of love … It's so pure!'[27]

Those few words must have consoled and strengthened Marie after her sister's death that occurred a few days later. Very soon, Mother Agnès of Jesus began working on what would become 'Story of a Soul', which replaced the death notice that was sent round to the Carmels on the death of a sister. Lisieux Carmel could not have anticipated the effect this book would have, because in a short while they were inundated from letters that would soon come from all over the world.

Marie became one of those who answered the letters because she was Thérèse's godmother and therefore had a special place among those who knew Thérèse best. She developed an extended group of friends and benefactors of the community and what she had once approached with trepidation, Thérèse's Act of Oblation, became the lodestone of her spiritual life and the message that she promoted most earnestly. It gradually transformed her character, a character that was at once lively and vivacious but at the same time reserved. She could sometimes speak without thinking, and Mother Agnès, who was so different in character, weighing things up first, pondering deeply, sometimes had to step in and rectify her 'gaffes'.

As the Cause for Thérèse's beatification and canonisation progressed, Marie was called to give her evidence, and shared in the community celebrations as their youngest sister was raised to the altars. After the festivities of the canonisation, Mother Agnès asked each sister to say what grace they had received. Marie's was the briefest; she had failed to die before the canonisation, as she had wished, and came out with this spirited response: 'You haven't bothered yourself with my infirmities, so you won't be the first I will greet!'

Marie, like all of the Martin sisters, did not enjoy going to the parlour and facing the adulation of being the godmother and one of the sisters of a saint, and with her quick wit often had a quick retort to offer, such as her remark about Mother Geneviève.

Love does ask things of the one loved, and the reason why Marie had expected to die before Thérèse's canonisation was that she began to suffer increasingly from rheumatoid arthritis, which over the years became more and more crippling and painful. It was a severe trial of love and acceptance to Marie that she, who had always been so active, independent and energetic, should find herself more and more incapacitated. On 29 April 1923, the arthritis attacked her muscles and she found herself even more constricted in her ability to function normally.

The following year she suffered from severe pneumonia, so much so that the community thought she might die, but Marie knew her time had not yet come. There were more years of suffering to come, and on 25 January 1929 she was moved to the infirmary and was confined to a wheelchair. Her legs and feet became swollen and she was riddled with sores. The Act of Oblation became the indispensable anchor in her suffering, which she offered for souls. When the pain became too much for her, she would cry from the pain but at the same time for her yearning for the conversion of souls, saying: 'Prayer is the state of my soul, I cry to the good God day and night: "My God, come to my aid. Hasten! Hasten to help me!" '. Her increasing immobility also became her 'weapon' in her desire for souls, as she said, 'I am as one in chains. I am fettered and constrained; my arms pain me. But I offer this to the good God in order that some poor soul may not be fettered and lost for all eternity'. However great her suffering, she never lost her trust in the *good* God whom she loved with an ever greater passion.

Marie celebrated her Golden Jubilee 15 October 1936, and the sisters gave her a watercolour painting of Thérèse crowning her on the day of her Profession, signed with an autograph from Pope Pius XI.

On 8 March 1937 Marie received the sacrament of Extreme Unction, but she carried on for another two years. In the June of 1939 she wrote her last letter to Léonie in Caen: 'We shall go together side by side to heaven, and the road is so long that we feel the effects of the journey. Which of us shall enter heaven first? It will probably be I, the most infirm'. Then, echoing Thérèse's own abandonment to the will of God so many years before, as to how long her sufferings would last, she continued: 'But I am unwilling to ask anything of the good God, for now more than ever we have the opportunities of saving souls. That is worth the pain of remaining here on earth for years more, if He wills it.' Her illness could have turned her in on herself, but it did not. She looked outward, to souls, to a world which needed her prayer and suffering. The Carmel would not have been cut off from news of a world that was moving inexorably towards war.

In the latter part of 1939 she contracted a cold with a bad cough which turned into pulmonary congestion. She made her final confession during January 1940, and on 18 January she appeared to be in a trance. She spoke very little, but when she did it was always about others: 'Souls! Souls!… There are so many who do not love the good God! Oh, how sad it all is!… Ah, how is it possible not to love so powerful, so great, so good a God Who does all for our welfare? Were I to go to hell, I would say to Him throughout eternity, My God, I love you!' The following day her last audible words were, 'I love You!' as she kissed her crucifix. At 2.30, while she was renewing her Act of Oblation her gaze fixed on the statue of 'Our Lady of the Smile' which years before Thérèse had gazed on and received healing, Marie bowed her head and died. She was seventy nine years old.

The community were struck by the look of great peace and joy that lingered on her face. In the days that followed, the sisters were aware of mysterious perfumes that filled the air. She was laid to rest in a vault 23 January. The death notice, the circular that was sent to other Carmels, spoke of her in loving and generous terms:

Broken by rheumatism and crippled with pain, the dear 'godmother' retained to the end, together with her witty originality, her valiant courage, her passion for souls without any pose. She calmly faced the divine tryst, which she liked to call 'the day of great mercy'.

Her sister Pauline found an envelope addressed to her from Marie after her death and read it in tears. In it, Marie wrote to her beloved sister that she would spend her eternity making God known:

> the only true God, and Him who He has sent. Eternity is not long enough for us to know the infinite goodness of the good God, His infinite power, His infinite mercy, His infinite love for us. These are our eternal delights, which will never be exhausted. Our heart is made to understand them and to be nourished by them. My only desire is to lose myself in Him.

Marie entered Carmel perhaps an unwilling prisoner of the walls that confined her. She was even more of a prisoner during the years of her incapacitating illness, but she, who so longed for freedom, found that freedom in the boundless love of the good God. 'I have found Jesus within these four walls,' she said, 'and finding Him, I have found heaven.' It was Thérèse's Act of Oblation, which she recited over and over until it became part of her, which set her free to love and to give herself for souls. She was a true disciple of her youngest sister, her godchild. 'We are happy to die after having spent our life in loving,' she said.[28]

Notes

1 I. F. Gorrës, *The Hidden Face* (London: Burns & Oates, 1959), p. 38.
2 Thérèse of Lisieux, *Letters Vol 1.* (Washington DC: ICS Publications, 1982), translated by J. Clarke OCD p. 112.
3 Thérèse of Lisieux, *Story of a Soul* (Washington DC: ICS Publications, 1976), translated by J. Clarke OCD, p. 34.
4 *Ibid.*, p. 88.
5 Thérèse of Lisieux, *Letters Vol 1.*, p. 251, note 2.
6 *Ibid.*, p. 245.
7 *Ibid.*, p. 227.
8 *Ibid.*, p. 250.
9 *Ibid.*, p. 253.
10 *Ibid.*, p. 247.
11 *Ibid.*, p. 428, note 6.
12 Lisieux Carmel, *The Foundation of the Carmel of Lisieux and its Foundress Reverend Mother Geneviève of St Teresa 1913* (USA: Kessinger Publishing, 2007), (facsimile), translated by a Religious of the Society of the Holy Child Jesus, p. 110.
13 *Ibid.*
14 Thérèse of Lisieux, *Letters Vol 1.*, p. 433.
15 C. O'Mahoney OCD (ed.), *St Therese of Lisieux by Those Who Knew Her* (Dublin: Veritas Publications, 1975), pp. 96-97.
16 *Ibid.*, p. 83.
17 Thérèse of Lisieux, *Letters Vol 11.* (Washington DC: ICS Publications, 1988), translated by J. Clarke OCD, p 100, note 6.
18 *Ibid.*, pp. 991-993.
19 O'Mahoney, *Those Who Knew Her*, p. 96.
20 Thérèse of Lisieux, *Story of a Soul*, p. 193.
21 Thérèse of Lisieux, *Letters Vol 11.*, p. 997.
22 *Ibid.*, p. 999.
23 *Ibid.*
24 Gorrës, *The Hidden Face*, p. 100
25 P. Martin, (Mother Agnès of Jesus), *St Thérèse of Lisieux, Her Last Conversations* (Washington DC: ICS Publications 1977), translated by J. Clarke OCD, p. 238.
26 *Ibid.*, p. 243.
27 *Ibid.*
28 See additional material at *www.martinsisters.org*.

2

MOTHER AGNÈS OF JESUS

PAULINE MARTIN

WHEN THÉRÈSE, ON the day their mother was buried, flung herself into the arms of Pauline, claiming her as her mother, she was to be 'mother' to Thérèse in two ways, as that surrogate mother and, in Carmel, as her Prioress for three years.

Pauline was born 7 February 1861, almost a year after Marie, and was named after her aunt, Pauline Guérin. She was the daughter most like her mother both in character and looks, with lovely brown hair and eyes. She had a gentler character than Marie, affectionate and sensitive, with a soft voice, but with a stubborn streak, and was as energetic as Marie. Her father's nickname for her was 'Pearl', and she did indeed resemble that soft and brilliant gem.

When their mother sent Marie and Pauline to the Visitation convent for their schooling, Pauline proved to be an even better scholar than her elder sister. She discovered that she had a pronounced artistic talent, and when she was at home used the attic as her studio, painting in water colours; her father would bring back from his business travels shells, ivory and parchment on which she would paint delicate miniatures. She was also learning how to sew and embroider and she was learning the lacemaking at which her mother was so adept. She studied her catechism hard to prepare herself for her First Holy Communion, which she made 2 July 1847.

At the Visitation, Sister Marie-Dosithée became a surrogate mother to the two girls, but Pauline, especially, was the one closest to her. Pauline was heartbroken when Marie- Dosithée died from tuberculosis 24 February 1877, the last year of her stay at the Visitation; the sadness of this year was made even darker when in July her mother was diagnosed with cancer of the breast. Zélie was comforted with the thought that she was leaving her family in good hands with Marie and Pauline, but it was Pauline whom she saw as the mother of the youngest girls. 'You are my true friend,' she wrote to Pauline. 'You give me courage to endure life with patience. Be always the joy to others that you have been to me. The good God will bless you not only in the next world, but in this, because he is always happiest, even in this life, with those who always bravely do their duty.'

In hope for a cure, Zélie decided to go to Lourdes. There was a group going from Angers, so Zélie, Marie and Léonie set off on 18 June, picking up Pauline from Le Mans on the way. The pilgrimage was not a success. On the train journey, a pot of coffee spilt over their luggage, ruining both their clothes and the food they had brought with them. Arriving at Lourdes, they found the hotel they had booked was totally unsuitable and so had to look for another one. Zélie endured daily baths in the ice cold water of the baths, but it was obvious that she would receive no physical cure. The party returned home to prepare themselves for their mother's death.

Their mother's one concern was that, however talented her daughters were, they should have a strong faith, and Pauline strove hard to fulfil her mother's expectations. Her mother was very keen that her daughters would become nuns, but at one point it seemed that only the least likely one, Léonie, would fulfil her desires. As for Marie and Pauline, Zélie wrote to her brother that, 'for the two oldest girls, here are their thoughts: Marie doesn't want to hear a word about the convent, and she wants to remain an old maid. Pauline wants neither the convent nor marriage, nor to remain an old maid—and I don't know how she'll be able to manage that!'[1] Pauline was, however, quietly undergoing a change of heart and found herself increasingly drawn to the religious life. She took it for granted that she would enter the Visitation Order, but God had other plans for her. On the morning of 16 February 1877 she went to the 6 o'clock Mass at St Jacques, which was being celebrated in the side chapel of Our Lady of Mount Carmel. 'Suddenly there was a very vivid light within my soul,' she recalled. 'The good God showed me clearly that He didn't want me at the Visitation but in Carmel.' She remembered a very dear friend who had died the previous year, who had spoken to Pauline of her desire to enter Carmel and to take the name of Agnès of Jesus, with the implication that this was the name she should take. This sudden revelation made her blush so much with emotion that when she went up to receive communion she felt sure that others would notice.

Quietly she began to prepare to leave her beloved family, but she kept this intention from Thérèse, who was now nine years old. Thérèse found out only by chance, overhearing a conversation, and was devastated. Pauline took her aside and explained something of the life of Carmel to her; the young girl immediately felt that this was what she wanted for herself, too. It was the seed of Thérèse's vocation. However, Pauline, so engrossed in following her own calling, didn't understand the depths of Thérèse's distress at losing another mother.

Pauline entered Carmel 2 October 1882, and on the same day Thérèse started school at the Benedictine Abbey in Lisieux. Pauline was accompanied by her father, Marie and her uncle to the Carmel, where they heard Mass. Her spiritual director, Abbé Ducellier, spoke a few words, and then the cloister door opened to receive her.

The following day, Mother Geneviève of Saint Teresa, the monastery's foundress, noticed how pale she was and asked her if she was sad. Pauline, now Sister Agnès, admitted that she was, and when asked why, replied, 'I think I've entered Carmel old,' a remark that perhaps reflected the fact that many of the other nuns were elderly, and none of her own age.

However, she quickly adapted to her new life, embracing the austerities and the joys of the life with equal enthusiasm. Her Novice Mistress was Sister Marie of the Angels, the same Mistress that Thérèse would have when she entered. She 'was really a saint, the product of the first Carmelites', was Thérèse's description of her after her entry, but added, 'Her kindness towards me was limitless and still my soul did not expand under her direction.' Pauline had the same problem, because however well-meaning Mary of the Angels was, the nun tired her greatly with her unceasing questions. She did, however, introduce Sister Agnès to the devotion to the Holy Face, a devotion that was spreading from the Poitiers Carmel, from which the Lisieux Carmel had been founded, and which would have such an influence on Thérèse later. Agnès blossomed under the peaceable and luminous influence of the saintly former Prioress, who was more of an influence on her than her Novice Mistress, and whose peace passed into the soul of her postulant.

Mother Marie de Gonzague gave permission for the family, including the Guérins, to visit Sister Agnès each Thursday. When these visits only added to Thérèse's distress and alienation, and she was allowed only a couple of minutes at the end of the visit to speak to her 'little mother' herself, Sister Agnès still did not understand the depths of Thérèse's distress; all she saw was her young sister's tears for which she scolded her: 'You distressed me this morning,' she wrote to her in November, 'when you were crying like a *baby!* But since I've already preached to you and *scolded* you, I must now act as the indulgent sister, isn't that so?'[2] She went on to urge Thérèse to accept the sacrifice of her absence, which Agnès felt only too much herself. Later, she bitterly regretted not understanding her young sister's heartbreak:

> I used to be very sad when Thérèse cried at the end of Marie's visits. But how was I to console her! I was unaware of the abyss of sadness that formed in her soul at my departure. I understand very well now how the five minutes given to her with me could only cause her more anguish. And, then, I was so foolish that with all my politeness to my aunt when she came with my cousins! Céline and Thérèse no longer counted; all my attention was centred on the other side.
>
> And yet I believed I was acting well, and that Marie was going to understand me and have

> my poor little Thérèse understand me, in whose eyes I always used to see tears forming! And a little pout which would show whenever she tried to refrain from crying any more. Ah! Once again, if only I had known![3]

Elections were held 31 January 1883 and brought in various changes. Mother Geneviève of St Teresa was re-elected Prioress, Mother Marie of the Angels became Sub-Prioress, and Mother Marie de Gonzague became Novice Mistress. Mother de Gonzague was a complex character, and Sister Agnès, as her novice, became more aware of her shortcomings. Both the Prioress and her Novice Mistress soon recognised her talent for painting, and gave her many commissions for painting little holy cards and other mementos that helped towards the community's finances, a great blessing for a very poor Carmel with limited resources. She also had a talent for composing poems, which was brought into play for celebrating the various happenings in Carmel—Clothings, Professions, anniversaries.

Agnès was worried by the severe headaches that Thérèse developed, but when Lent began, writing and visits were suspended for the penitential season, only broken on 13 March when she wrote to tell her father that she had been accepted to receive the habit, with the ceremony set for Friday 6 April 1883.

On 25 March, Easter night, her uncle disturbed Thérèse so much by reminiscing on memories he had of her mother, that she entered into a more disturbing phase of her illness, having seizures and hallucinations.

Told of her little sister's illness, Sister Agnès could only pray and encourage her, writing her long letters of consolation, and, realising now how Thérèse had suffered from lack of attention during the family's visits to her, promised her a long visit all of her own when she got better. Thérèse made a great effort to be well enough to go to her Clothing ceremony. Agnès, as was the custom, came out of the cloister in her white dress to be with her family, and Thérèse was able to embrace her before she went back into the cloister to receive the habit. Thérèse had a serious relapse the following day and it was not until Pentecost, 13 May that she was cured by the vision of Our Lady of the Smile.

With Thérèse now cured, Sister Agnès was more at peace. She was given permission to make an elaborate and profusely decorated little book for Thérèse, to prepare her for her First Holy Communion. This was to be 8 May 1884, which was also the date set for Sister Agnès' Profession. Although Lent began 27 February, Agnès was given permission to write a weekly letter to her sister as an additional guidance during this period of preparation.

The book prepared Thérèse for the three months leading to the great day, with a page a day in which Thérèse would write down her acts of self-denial, her acts of virtue, her 'aspirations', short prayers to God. The heroic nature of the eleven year old child's preparations did not occur to Agnès: during the sixty eight days Thérèse made 1,949 acts of self-denial and of virtue. On the day before her First Holy Communion she said 2,773 invocations, such as 'Little Jesus, I love you', that Agnès had suggested to her. Using the affectionate nickname for Thérèse that Mother Marie de Gonzague also used, she wrote 6 May 'I see that Therésita is preparing her heart well for the great day. You must continue and not stop for an instant, for one instant lost is a flower less in the little garden.'[4]

In the afternoon of her First Communion, Thérèse went to the Carmel to see her sister in her white veil crowned with flowers, matching her own white dress. That morning, in the oratory of the Blessed Sacrament, Agnès had pronounced her vows at the hands of her Prioress. Seeing her young sister with a radiant and calm peace on her face, it consoled Agnès that Thérèse was truly restored to both physical and spiritual health. 'She looked at me with such a profound and gentle air', she recalled, 'I left the parlour wholly reassured, a little like the Apostles as they came down from the mount of Tabor.' The following month, 16 July, Feast of Our Lady of Mount Carmel, Agnès received the black veil of her Profession.

There were fresh elections in 1886; Mother Geneviève was now too ill to continue as Prioress, and Mother de Gonzague again took up the post; Mother Marie of the Angels became Novice Mistress once more. As was customary, Agnès remained in the novitiate for a further three years after her Profession, and when Marie entered 15 October 1886, Feast of St Teresa of Avila, Mother de Gonzague appointed her as Marie's 'angel'.

She was well able to encourage her elder sister who was somewhat daunted by the austerity of Carmel, which Agnès herself, who had always been inclined to embrace austerity of life, had not felt difficult. She encouraged Marie to return at each moment to the source, Jesus, who gave meaning to their life. 'Come, and with the lamb, drink that water which springs up to eternal life. Have no tears in your eyes any more, because all things are passing. Love Jesus, very much, because he will never fail you. Be the first in everything, the most faithful in everything.' Agnès left the novitiate the following year 21 June 1887, to take her place in the community as a full Chapter sister.

The following year, 9 April 1888, Thérèse entered Carmel. Sister Agnès was the refectorian, charged with laying out the bread and water on the tables, and keeping the refectory clean and dusted. Mother Marie de Gonzague appointed Thérèse as her assistant, assuming, as she had with Marie, that the two sisters would talk with each other, so that Agnes could give extra help to her youngest sister as she adjusted to Carmelite life. When Thérèse again refused to avail herself of this relaxation and kept steadfastly to the rules of silence, this made a strain in the relationship between the two, and Thérèse later said to her that 'You had come to the point where you no longer knew me'. But Thérèse was determined that she had to break those ties of family within the cloister, for all the sisters were her family now.

On 8 September 1890, Thérèse was professed, and received the black veil on the 24th, although her father was too ill to attend. Thérèse was in tears over her disappointment, and Agnès, not understanding the stress she was under, scolded her for her childishness over thinking her father would be able to be there.

The winter of 1891 was an exceptionally severe one and the foundress, Mother Geneviève, died 5 December. Later that month the community was laid low with the influenza that swept through the country and two more sisters died. Only Thérèse and Sister Martha were unaffected and kept going the running of the house. In January the epidemic died down gradually, but because the community was still recovering and mourning the loss of the sisters, the elections, which were due in February, were postponed for a year and

Mother Marie de Gonzague continued as Prioress. Since she had been in office for six years, serving a double term, she was ineligible to stand again when the elections eventually took place 20 February 1893; Sister Agnès was elected Prioress.

Her aunt wrote[5] to her daughter Jeanne to tell her the news that day, after her husband, Céline, Léonie and Marie Guérin had visited Agnès, now Mother Agnès, in the parlour. She wrote how her niece was in tears, 'for a heavy weight has fallen upon her shoulders, young as she is'—Agnès was thirty one years old. Her letter witnesses to the delicate situation that would make this, her first period as Prioress, such a heavy and fraught burden. 'The visit of the young girls was not gay', Mme Guérin wrote, 'and this even more so because the situation was very delicate for them. Mother Marie de Gonzague was present, and this required much tact.' Perhaps the visitors could not show too much delight at the election of 'one of their own' while the outgoing Prioress was there.

It would even be difficult to write to Agnès, because 'I think, dear Jeanne, it will be good for you to write her a little letter, but you should keep in mind that Mother Marie de Gonzague may see it, and so you should keep a certain reserve.' An editorial note to this letter says that this was because Mother Agnès would undoubtedly have had to show it to her. When Mother Marie de Gonzague tried to cling on to power by continuing to read the letters, both those coming in and those being sent, Mother Agnès had to go so far as to hide herself to read letters without the older nun wanting to see them, too. She had a special arrangement with Céline: 'Be sure to address your letters always to Mother Marie de Gonzague,' she wrote to her. 'You will be receiving a letter addressed to me. I beg you not to send it to me but to bring it yourself. It mustn't go into Mother Marie de Gonzague's mail bag.'

It would take some time for the new Prioress to have the courage to assert her independence from the old Prioress's influence. As Mme Guérin pointed out, 'It is certain that our dear little Pauline has everything necessary to make a good superior, but she is so timid, so easily moved, her health is weak and she is very young. Once she has overcome her feelings and has been broken into her charge, I am sure she will be all right.'

This insight might be said to define Agnès' first period as Prioress. Mother Marie de Gonzague had championed her election because she thought that Agnès was malleable enough for her to be under the thumb of the older nun. Confident of being re-elected at the next election, it was a way of being in actual charge until then, with Agnès doing her bidding. There would be frightful ructions when this did not transpire—when Agnès did indeed find her own feet as Prioress.

In her letter Mme Guérin said that 'our little Pauline was elected by unanimous vote', but this was not so. It is a measure of the laxness in the community that what was supposed to be a secret ballot was not secret at all. In fact, the community's vote was divided, because some sisters resented what they saw as the 'Martin clan', with three sisters from the same family in the community, something that would become even more pronounced when Céline and Marie Guérin, their cousin, would also enter. This was in addition to the rancour over the many gifts that M Martin showered on the community.

At the time, there were only three sisters in the Novitiate, Thérèse and two lay sisters, Martha of Jesus and Mary Magdalen of the Blessed Sacrament. Mother Marie of the Angels had been elected Subprioress, and so Mother Agnès appointed Mother Marie de Gonzague as Novice Mistress. However, knowing from her own experience during her novitiate the nun's unstable and erratic character, she asked Thérèse to keep a discreet eye on her two fellow novices. Mother Marie de Gonzague agreed to the arrangement, that Thérèse would aid her in correcting and sometimes instructing her companions. In effect, she became assistant Novice Mistress without the title, and it needed all her tact and discernment to train the two novices, who often resented her guidance; at the same time Thérèse remained under Mother Marie de Gonzague's authority and had to carry out these duties without usurping her position. Mother Agnès had now seen in her youngest sister, who was only twenty years old, sufficient maturity and spiritual development to feel confident that she could tread such a delicate tightrope.

When another postulant entered 16 June 1894, taking the name of Marie of the Trinity, Thérèse was also given to her as her 'angel' but with a role that effectively made Thérèse her novice mistress.

Thérèse herself was understandably delighted that her beloved sister was yet again her 'little Mother'—'little', because Mother Agnès was petite compared to her sisters, especially Thérèse, who was tall and well built. Now, her sister was her mother in a new way; years before, though, Thérèse had said that she wanted to enter Carmel, not in order to be closer to her sister, but for God alone, and she now used her iron control to live that out. The sisters were supposed to meet the Prioress once a month to speak of their spiritual life, but often Thérèse did not avail herself even of this legitimate time to be with her sister.

With her deep respect for the office of Prioress, in which the superior expressed the will of God for her, she was deeply hurt by the conflicts between Mother Agnès and Mother Marie de Gonzague, which often rocked the community. However, she also saw that these trials could be a source of joy, because they matured her sister, and gave her a way of sharing in the Cross of Christ.

The biggest eruption occurred over Céline's Profession. She had entered 14 September 1895, after their father's death 29 July, was clothed 5 February, and was therefore due to make her Profession the following year. However, Mother Agnès' term of office was due to end in February, and Mother Marie de Gonzague, who expected to be elected, wanted the Profession delayed so that Céline, now Sister Geneviève of the St Teresa, would make her vows at her hands. Sister Marie of the Trinity was also due to be professed, Marie Guérin, now Sister Marie of the Eucharist, was due to be clothed in the habit, and she wanted all those events to take place under her term of office.

She got her way over Marie of the Trinity's profession, which was delayed until after the elections, but she had other ways of humiliating Mother Agnès, making her stay outside the door when the Chapter sisters voted to accept Sister Geneviève for profession, a gross abuse of power. Further, she was planning to send the newly professed sister to the foundation of Saigon in order to water down the influence the Martin sisters had in the community. All this was being discussed while the sisters were at the wash one day in January, and Sister Aimée of Jesus, one of those most opposed to the 'Martin clan', declared that Mother Marie de Gonzague had every right to test Geneviève, as she was the Novice Mistress. Then a clear voice arose from an unexpected quarter; 'There are some trials which one does not have the right to impose.' It was Thérèse speaking, the only time she spoke a word of criticism of her Prioress.

Elections took place on 21 March 1896, and Mother Marie de Gonzague was indeed elected after seven ballots, with a majority of one. Of that first time as Prioress Mother Agnès wrote much later: 'She wouldn't allow me to have too much authority. She wanted me to be at all times under her domination. That's what I had to endure and cried over during those three years! But I recognise that this was necessary. It matured me and detached my soul from honours.'

However difficult her time as Prioress was, during those years the community changed a great deal, especially with the influx of new vocations. There were five sisters in the Novitiate by the time her term of office came to an end, which injected much needed new and young blood into what had been an ageing community. It also covered a period of her youngest sister's rapid advance in holiness. Thérèse had written the account of her childhood; training the young novices had given flesh to her 'Little Way'; Mother Agnès had given her permission to make her Act of Oblation, and a few days later Thérèse had received the experience of being plunged into a fire of love. She had also given her a spiritual brother, abbe Bellière.

All of this happened while Mother Agnès was her superior and therefore knew what had taken place, but she still did not really understand the profundity of it, especially the importance of the dart of love Thérèse had experienced. Thérèse said as much a couple of months before she died.

Thérèse had given her the manuscript of what would become the first book of 'Story of a Soul' the day before her Feast Day of St Agnes in January, but due to the pressures of her duties as Prioress it remained unread. She finally got round to reading it a few weeks after the elections and was astounded at what she found there. Agnès knew Thérèse had been a very pious little girl, but this manuscript revealed that her little sister was exceptional.

That Feast Day was not a happy occasion, with the tensions in the community and the elections looming. One indication of this occurred during the play Thérèse had written for the occasion, on the Flight into Egypt. Mother Agnès found it far too long and cut it short half way through, leaving Thérèse to cry in private over the snub.

In the Lisieux Carmel it was the custom for the outgoing Prioress to be nominated Novice Mistress, but Mother Marie de Gonzague further humiliated Mother Agnès and ignored this, keeping the role for herself. Mother Agnès was elected as a Councillor and was given the post of Depositrix, the sister in charge of the finances, accounts and supplies. It was a definite demotion. However, the new Prioress had experienced the way in which Thérèse had conducted herself as her assistant in the Novitiate and gave her an official title as Assistant Novice Mistress. With all the responsibilities Mother Marie de Gonzague now had, it meant that Thérèse was, in effect, Novice Mistress. Despite her faults, it showed that the Prioress had discernment and had appreciated the way in which Thérèse had carried out a very difficult task.

That Mother Agnès did not have this greater responsibility herself turned out to be providential. On the eve of Maundy Thursday Thérèse coughed up blood, a signal of the rapid deterioration of her health. Because Mother Agnès was no longer Prioress, Thérèse did not tell her, although if she had sought permission to do so it would have been granted. She did not want her beloved sister to know the full gravity of the situation, and hid her condition so well, because she knew the distress it would cause her. Mother Agnès had already been distressed enough at reading Thérèse's poem 'To live by love' with its yearning for death.

When Thérèse was finally admitted to the infirmary the following year, Agnès was free to be with her sister as much as possible, and, realising her holiness and the importance of her account of her spiritual journey, began writing down the conversations she had with her youngest sister during these final months of her life. These reminiscences were revealing, not only for the heroism with which Thérèse lived out these last few, harrowing months of her life, but also Agnès's lack of understanding of her youngest sister's 'Little Way'. She had brought Thérèse up to count her acts of virtue and self-denial, to add pearls to her crown, but Thérèse, however well this approach helped her in her early years, had passed far beyond this type of spirituality into an entirely new realm. Agnès was unable to see further than that one had to come to God with the merits amassed during a lifetime of self-denial and love of God: 'When I come to die, alas, I shall have nothing to give to God', she remarked to Thérèse, 'and that troubles me deeply.' 'It is just the reverse with me', was Thérèse's spirited response. 'If I had all the works of St Paul to offer, I would still feel myself to be an unprofitable servant; I would still consider that my hands were empty. But that is precisely what gives me joy, for since I have nothing I must receive everything from God.'[6]

Several times Agnès would ask her about the manner of her death; would she prefer living to dying, or dying on a great Feast Day or the anniversary of the reception of the Veil? Again, Thérèse was totally abandoned to the will of God; in any case, the day of her death would itself be a feast for her, she said, when she would be going into the full vision and presence of the One she had loved so passionately.

That day arrived 29 September 1897. Even before Thérèse's death, Mother Agnès had decided that she would make into a book the account Thérèse had written of her early life, together with the letter she had written to Sister Marie of the Sacred Heart and the 'treatise' on charity written for Mother Marie de Gonzague, to send round to the Carmels instead of the obituary. To mollify the Prioress, all of it would be presented as if written to her. Thérèse, before her death, had agreed to the publication, because she realised that it would do good to souls and spread her teachings; she had also said to Mother Agnès that she could make any changes she wanted. Mother Agnès proceeded to do so and changed Thérèse's thought almost beyond recognition. It was not until the unedited edition of Thérèse's writings was published that people were able to read what she had actually written. Despite this, the book had astounding success and letters began to pour into the monastery from all over the world, telling of lives changed and miracles occurring.

Did Mother Agnès ever really understand her young sister's teaching and holiness totally? That she changed Thérèse's manuscript so much says not, although some of the changes were because she felt some recollections of their family life were too intimate for general distribution. She also suppressed some passages that she felt detracted from the holiness of her sister that she wanted to promote, such as the fact that Marie was still combing Thérèse's hair at the age of eleven. Brought up in a milieu that put great emphasis on works and sacrifice, it was very difficult for her to break free of that training, and with her innate timidity, to launch herself fully, as Thérèse did, on the waves of confidence and love. It is interesting that in her talks to the community as their Prioress she rarely referred to Thérèse's words or example, considering that it was not suitable for Carmelites![7] Instead, she drew heavily on other spiritual writers, especially her beloved Francis de Sales.

Mother Marie de Gonzague's last term of office, with Mother Agnès as Subprioress, came to an end in 1902, and Agnès was again elected Prioress, a post she held for the next six years. In her first homily to the community after her election, she said to them:

> When you want to come to me I will try not to betray your confidence. I know well that I am only a feeble instrument in the hands of the good God. If you think of me as the good God's little bell, without considering whether this little bell is made of brass or gold, whether it rings true or false, I tell you that it is Jesus and not someone else who will respond to your request, whether it is for your instruction, or to test you, whether to reprove or console you.[8]

She had all the qualities of a good superior of the time; she was imbued with the spirit of the austere Carmelite

Rule, but tempered by the spirit of St Francis de Sales, a saint whose writings and spirituality she treasured above all. With simplicity and delicacy, she encouraged her sisters to walk 'the path of asceticism and the practice of the moral virtues.' With a deep love of the Mass and the presence of Jesus in the Eucharist, she encouraged her sisters to have an exalted respect for each other:

> So what is there in common, at the altar, between a piece of bread and God? That this example should impel us to treat our sisters with like love and tenderness. If a sister is a rich tabernacle, let us bless our Lord for this. If in another, on the other hand, it seems to us that this God of love is less at home there, there is even more reason for us to adore him and love him there even more than elsewhere.[9]

During her time as Prioress she saw the volume of letters increase to a staggering number day by day, with requests for relics, pictures and holy cards. Sister Geneviève's talents for art came in very useful in fulfilling these requests. At one point Mother Agnès, with Mother Marie de Gonzague, left the enclosure on business; this excursion gave them the opportunity to see and to pray at Thérèse's tomb, at that time in the public cemetery, which was becoming an ever greater magnet to the pilgrims who were making their way to Lisieux. It also gave them the opportunity to go to the Visitation convent at Caen to visit a radiant Léonie who had entered the Caen community for the last and definitive time, just as Thérèse had prophesied before her death. Léonie had received a copy of 'Story of a Soul' and was finding it a revelation of her young sister as well as a sure path to the holiness she craved. When she made her Profession 14 May 1900, Mother Agnès made it a day of rejoicing for the Lisieux community as well, and because of Léonie's presence at the Visitation, there grew up a firm bond between the two communities..

Shortly after she let go of the reins of office, Mother Marie de Gonzague was diagnosed with cancer of the tongue. The bitterness between the two was now gone. 'She loved me as far as she was able', Mother Agnès testified, 'and I loved her with a sincere and disinterested love, recognising in a way she certainly had, in the ascendancy she had over the sisters, even over the convent's Superior, that enabled all four of us and Sister Marie of the Eucharist, to be received into the Carmel.'

At this point no-one thought about the possibility of Thérèse's canonisation, until, in 1903, a young Scottish priest, Thomas Taylor, who had fallen under Thérèse's spell, came to the Lisieux parlour and said, 'You must think of canonising this saint!' Laughing, Mother Marie de Gonzague replied, 'So, how many Carmelites should be canonised!'

But the seed had been planted; Mother Agnès began to think seriously about it, but was deterred by the negative response from some Carmels—like Mother Marie de Gonzague, many prioresses considered that Thérèse was no holier than many of those in their own communities. Agnès discussed it with the bishop of Bayeux, Mgr Lemonnier, who was equally against the idea, so she spoke no more of it, leaving it to God.

Her second term of office came to an end in 1908, and on 8 May a young Professed sister still in the Novitiate, Sister Marie-Ange, was elected Prioress. She was the first to enter after Thérèse's death, and said she owed her vocation to her. Profoundly convinced of Thérèse's sanctity, Mother Marie-Ange approached the bishop once again, and, perhaps because she was not a family member of the Martins, and contrary to all expectation, this time the bishop gave his consent to institute a diocesan tribunal which opened in 1909.

It seems that this was all that Mother Marie-Ange's role was to be, because after only eighteen months as Prioress she died, and Mother Agnès was re-elected. Her life would never be the same again. With the progress of Thérèse's beatification and canonisation gathering pace, the community had to prepare their depositions and testify at the tribunals. Sackloads of mail poured in from all parts of the world, with even more requests for pictures, relics and requests for prayer, as well as accounts of miraculous answers to prayer through Thérèse's intercession. Mother Agnès found that she had a new role, answering letters from people needing spiritual guidance. Thérèse's 'little Mother' now found herself the 'little mother' of a whole new family of souls all over the world. There is a photograph of her sitting in the garden writing, with letters scattered all around her. She had discovered that she had a facility for letter-writing, responding, herself, to many of the letters. She also became the 'little mother' to a series of popes who became devotees of Thérèse—Pope John XX111, when Cardinal Roncalli, for example, visited the Carmel.

Thérèse was beatified 29 April 1923, and two years later, 17 May, she was canonised. Her sisters were invited to attend the ceremonies at Rome, but declined, preferring to listen on the radio, surrounded by their community, the cloisters decorated and the sisters in festive mood. Two extern sisters represented them in Rome. On the day of Thérèse's beatification, Pope Pius X1 had an extra honour and distinction for Mother

Agnès, when he made her Prioress of the Lisieux Carmel for the rest of her life.

This gave the community the stability it needed when it seemed that the whole world was beating a path to Lisieux. It was her genius that with all the publicity that surrounded them, she was able to keep the community grounded in the primary function of their vocation, a life of loving reparation, prayer and self-denial for souls. She was practical, always able to see both sides of a problem, which meant that she could sometimes be indecisive, but growing into her role as Prioress gave her more confidence and made her more sure of herself. Calm, and peaceable, with a great capacity for hard work, she remained grounded in humility. None of the Martin sisters allowed the distinction of being the 'sisters of the Little Flower', sisters of a saint, to go to their heads. For all of them, Marie, Pauline, Léonie and Céline, their vocation as religious was of primary importance.

When the Carmelites had to leave their cloister for a few months during the Second World War, to take shelter in the crypt of the Basilica, they walked there with lowered veils to avoid the curiosity of the people. Mother Agnès helped them to observe the Rule as much as possible under these difficult circumstances. However, being obliged to leave their cloister gave the Martin sisters the opportunity of visiting Les Buissonets, which escaped the bombing, to see the much loved home of their childhood, and also the new resting place of Thérèse and the sisters who had died after her, in the cemetery.

The publicity surrounding Thérèse was not all positive. Since Thérèse had said to Mother Agnès that she should edit her writings as she saw fit, when theologians came to examine these edited writings the Prioress came in for much criticism, because of the ways they distorted Thérèse's own thought. Faced with this criticism, Mother Agnès agreed that her youngest sister's writings should be published in their original state, but only after her death.

Another criticism was that the Martin sisters were promoting Thérèse to enhance their family's standing, far beyond what was due to Thérèse's own holiness. However, all these setbacks could not halt the onward march of Thérèse's influence.

One symbol of this was the plan to build a basilica in her honour, which grew increasingly necessary to accommodate the flood of pilgrims. Céline found that she had a real gift for interpreting architects' plans, and on 11 July 1937, just before the 2nd World War, the basilica was consecrated by Cardinal Pacelli, the future Pope Pius X11. The Pope would remain a close friend of Mother Agnès, writing personally to her, asking for her prayers. In her later years, Mother Agnès's greatest pleasure was to see the spires of the basilica from her cell window and to unite her prayers to those of the countless pilgrims who flocked there, seeking the intercession of her youngest sister.

The timidity of her early years became a reticence that hid her inner life to a great extent from the outside world. In her homilies to her sisters in Chapter meetings she could reveal herself to some extent, but she was not able to rid herself all at once of her fear of God's judgement, despite Thérèse's influence. She recorded one terrifying occasion in 1932, during the Vigil of Sister Marie of the Incarnation's Clothing, when a ferocious storm outside mirrored an inner storm within her soul:

Our cell gave on to the street, which no longer exists today, and that evening, unfortunately, there was a violent storm. After Matins, I heard what sounded like a whirlwind, then a very loud noise that sounded as if part of the roof had fallen off into the road. I trembled so much my teeth were chattering and I couldn't stop. By the end of the day I wasn't able to contain my fear for it seemed like a nightmare. It was more than ordinary fear, it was such terror that it made me ill. Such weakness humiliated me, but what could I do? I prayed hard, but it did not free me. A maelstrom of feelings crushed me under the justice of God towards impenitent sinners, 'wandering stars for whom a tempest of shadows is reserved for all eternity'. This text always returned to me in times of mortal anguish.[10]

That final remark takes us into Agnès' inner life, when she sometimes endured times of spiritual darkness; did she, like Thérèse, sometimes go through a sense of alienation from the love of God that united her to those who rejected God?

Friend and spiritual mother of Popes, Bishops and Cardinals, Mother Agnès saw her role above all as mother of her sisters in Carmel. She was solicitous, above all, of the young novices and their progress in holiness. One of them asked permission to record the beautiful thoughts that she had had during prayer time, but Mother Agnès said, No; the best prayer was to remain in simplicity before the good God her Father, and leave beautiful thoughts to others. This was her theme—holiness was not some grand venture, but the simplicity of living under the loving gaze of the good God.

By the time the war ended in 1945, Mother Agnès had suffered her own losses—her elder sister, Marie of the Sacred Heart, had died in the January of 1940, Léonie in June 1941. Only Sister Geneviève remained, and the two sisters drew ever closer. Geneviève laughingly but truly, called them 'two old ladies', for she was seventy six and Mother Agnès eighty four. She had always suffered from winter coughs, flu and congestion, which became more serious with age. Then, in 1945, she had a nasty fall in the garden which severely weakened her. 'I am praying to the good God to give me strength,' she said, 'because I am feeling myself becoming weaker.'

In January 1947, she contracted a pulmonary infection. Well looked after, she recovered, but the sisters thought it best to transfer her to the infirmary, which, unlike the rest of the monastery, was heated. During this year, she was in the end too weak to continue writing the letters which were so much a part of her apostolate. Her Ruby Jubilee of Profession on 8 May was a quiet community affair, but little by little she was losing the use of her legs. Smiling, she said to a sister, 'I ask myself if there is something new I can offer up today.'

On 12 November the following year the sisters considered that her health had deteriorated to such a degree that she should receive the Anointing of the Sick. By now, it was the Subprioress who was in charge of the day to day running of the monastery. In December the community received the Constitution *Sponsa Christi,* in which the Pope invited the nuns to renew their vows. When the ceremony took place 19 March the following year, the sisters renewed their vows in the hands of their beloved Mother Agnès; the previous November she had been able to receive for the last time the vows of a choir novice.

'In my old age', she said, 'I understand much better the sufferings of my Saviour. I want to love the good God as he loves me.' As spring returned she was able to be taken into the garden, under the cloisters and to the oratory. 'I am like someone close to heaven', she said 'Jesus is leaving me a little longer on earth, but it is as if I am no longer there. I thirst for the waters of eternal life.'

She did not have much longer to wait. On 15 July 1951 it became obvious that the end was near. Her sister Geneviève remained close by her side, but she was no longer able to speak. Two days later she again received the Sacrament of the Sick, and on the 23rd, when the Pope heard of the state of her health he sent a telegram giving her his blessing 'through the fraternal intercession of Saint Thérèse'. She was no longer able to read it, but the sisters placed in on her chest for a while. Saturday, 28 July, her breathing changed and the community was summoned. Suddenly, her hands seized those of her infirmarians, her eyes opened and she gazed on her beloved daughters. Mother Subprioress recited Mother Agnès' favourite invocation: 'Jesus meek and humble of heart, make my heart like unto yours', and she gave a beautiful smile.

'My little Mother, all your children are here, with Sister Geneviève,' the Subprioress said, and the Prioress turned her head to look at them. Another sister prayed, 'Saint little Thérèse, pray for us', and Mother Agnès slipped peacefully away, to go to her good God, and also to her beloved little sister, who, in a reversal of roles and in her own way had become a spiritual mother to her.[11]

Notes

1 Z.. and L. Martin, *A Call to a Deeper Love* (New York: St Paul Publications, 2011), translated by Ann Connors Hess, edited by Dr France Renda, p. 141.

2 Thérèse of Lisieux, *Letters Vol 1.* (Washington DC: ICS Publications, 1982), translated by J. Clarke OCD p. 150.

3 *Ibid.*, p. 151.

4 *Ibid.*, p. 192.

5 Thérèse of Lisieux, *Letters Vol 11.* (Washington DC: ICS Publications, 1988), translated by J. Clarke OCD, p. 779.

6 I. F. Gorrës, *The Hidden Face* (London: Burns & Oates, 1959), pp. 278ff.

7 J. Vinatier, *Mère Agnès de Jesus* (Paris: Les Editions du Cerf, 1993), p. 121.

8 *Ibid.*, p. 119.

9 *Ibid.*, p. 120.

10 *Ibid.*, p. 182.

11 For additional material see *www.martinsisters.org*.

3

SISTER FRANÇOISE-THÉRÈSE

LEONIE MARTIN

THÉRÈSE LONGED TO be unknown, disregarded by all; in Carmel, when she went to the parlour with Marie and Pauline to see the Guérins, she hardly spoke at all, remaining discreetly at the side and leaving as soon as she could. It is true that in the monastery some of the sisters positively disliked her; she was sometimes the butt of a sharp tongue, but by others she was esteemed. Even though she remained in the Novitiate and never took her place in the Chapter, the fact that she was Novice Mistress in all but name gave her a certain standing in the community. She was attractive, intelligent and gifted, so it would have been easy for her to become proud. Her grounding in humility was to see all the gifts and graces that she acknowledged she had as coming totally from God's hands. Her humility was to understand deeply that she could boast of nothing as being hers.

What if one is not pretty, though, is awkward and unvalued, has learning difficulties, and has a troublesome personality? Such was the Martins' third surviving daughter, Léonie. Even her mother despaired of her. 'I cannot understand her character; the wisest sages would be out of their depth with her,' she wrote to her brother Isidore, to whom she poured out all that was happening in the household, and especially her troubles with Léonie. Being a pharmacist he could understand and perhaps help with remedies. 'Poor Léonie' was to be a favourite family epithet applied to one who was so different from her sisters that Léonie herself, in all earnestness, once wondered whether she was a changeling. Even her father, when he gave nicknames to his girls, could come up only with the epithet 'good', which was often not exactly what others would call her.

Born 8 June 1863, she was a sickly child and for many months there were fears that she would not survive. 'Little Léonie is over nine months old , and she can barely hold herself up on her legs as Marie was doing at three months old,' her mother wrote to her brother in 1864. 'This poor child is so weak. She has a kind of chronic whooping cough, fortunately not as strong as the attack Pauline had, as she wouldn't be able to survive it, and God only gives us what we can endure.'[1] She also had severe attacks of eczema, which troubled her all her life.

Her parents decided that, like Marie and Pauline, Léonie should be sent as a boarder to the convent at Le Mans, under the careful eye of Sister Marie Dorithée. The convent, however, insisted that she wait until she was a little older and could perhaps benefit more from the experience, since she was so backward in her studies. Léonie was delighted when at last she was allowed to go when she was nine years old, and her mother, knowing she would be in good hands, said that she felt as if she was in heaven.However, Zélie did not have an optimistic assessment of her young daughter, or how much she would be able to learn at the convent school: 'I only have one sorrow, not seeing my poor Léonie like [Marie]' she wrote again to her brother, 'What's more, I can't analyze her character; the most learned would be baffled by it. However, I hope the good seed will one day sprout up from the earth. If I see this, I'll sing my *Nunc Dimittis*.'[2]

Her mother could not help comparing her to her other girls, invariably to Léonie's detriment, and the poor girl could hardly fail to be aware of this. 'If you could only have seen the two eldest today,' she wrote to her brother, 'all dressed up; everyone admired them and could hardly take their eyes off them. I was radiant; I said to myself: "They are mine. I have two others who aren't here, one lovely and one less so—I love her as much as the others, but she won't be as much of a credit to me"'.[3] With rather brutal frankness her sister Pauline wrote to Léonie later in life: 'I shudder when I think of your childhood; you were a cuckoo in the nest.' Unprepossessing in appearance, unlike her sisters who were very pretty, with a prominent jaw of which Léonie was unhappily aware, she was rough and almost impossible to control, having a will of iron. She was, in fact, what would now be called a child with 'special needs'.

Zélie's expectations may have been heightened by her first two bright and intelligent daughters, but Sister Marie-Dorithée, with a born teacher's intuition, was able to see beneath her wildness and stubbornness, and was soon able to write to her parents:

> As you know, this poor child has many faults. The first month, I would scold her when she didn't do well, and this happened so frequently that I hardly did anything else… I could see that I was going to make this little girl unhappy, and that's not what I wanted to do, I wanted to be God's Providence with regard to her… So I

> began to treat her with the greatest gentleness, avoiding scolding her and telling her that I saw she wanted to be good and to please me, that I had faith in her … This had a magical effect on her, not only temporary but long lasting, because it is reasonable and I find her quite gentle.[4]

The Sister even went so far as to call her a 'predestined child' and said:

> She is a difficult child to train, and her childhood will not show any attractiveness, but I believe that eventually she will be as good as her sisters. She has a heart of gold, her intelligence is not yet developed, and she is far behind-hand for her age. Nevertheless, she does not lack capabilities, and I find that she has a good judgement and remarkable strength of character. In short, by nature she is strong and generous, quite to my taste. But if the grace of God were not there, what would become of her?'

Sadly, despite the Sister's optimistic opinion that such a transformation would last, with two attempts and after two years, placing her at Le Mans failed and she returned home, going instead to school at Alençon. Marie took over her studies, and her mother placed her with two nuns to give her extra lessons. This turned out to be disastrous, because the two ladies turned out not to be nuns at all. Further, an eight year old girl was staying with them, ostensibly so that they could look after her; instead, they were beating and starving her. When Zélie discovered this, she fought strenuously for the truth to come out, which even saw her asked to attend at the police station, until she saw the little girl back with her mother again.

Back at home, Léonie's behaviour became even more unpredictable and she refused to do anything that her mother asked. Her mother felt bitterly that she could not get through to her any more; Léonie did only what she wanted, when she wanted. She was covered, her mother said, with faults like a blanket. Her sullenness, wildness and rudeness which disrupted the whole household hurt her mother deeply and she was at a loss to know what to do with her. In the end, it was Marie who discovered the cause. While M Martin had to go away on frequent business trips and Mme Martin was absorbed in her lace-making business, Léonie was left to the mercy of one of their servants, Louise, who had a malign influence over the child. She bullied, blackmailed and ill-treated her, forcing Léonie to obey her rather than her mother. Once the dreadful truth came out, Zélie wanted to dismiss the servant and yielded to her pleas only on the understanding that she would never go near the child again, and that after her death, when she was no longer there to keep an eye on her, the servant should be dismissed. Louise later said that she bitterly regretted her treatment of Léonie, and said that the pain of regret never left her for the rest of her life.

Once freed from Louise's influence, Léonie now became a changed being, her good, generous and loving side began to emerge, and she almost obsessively clung to her mother. With her cancer spreading and causing her immense pain, Mme Martin worried about what would happen to Léonie after her death; Marie promised to take her place and under her wise and firm guidance Léonie continued to blossom according to her capacity.

While her mother could be assured that Marie would train her wisely, she still worried about what Léonie would do once she was grown up. Léonie herself had declared that she wanted to be a nun, which Zélie thought highly unlikely, though also highly desirable. At the Visitation school, despite her wildness, Léonie had begun to appreciate the kindly, gentle, Salesian spirit which drew her and began to have an influence on her, and it fostered within her a desire for the religious life. In the January of 1877 she became aware that her aunt was seriously ill, and decided she wanted to write to her. She wrote to Sister Marie-Dosithée: 'My dear Aunt, when you are in heaven, please ask God to give me the grace of conversion, and also give me a vocation to be a true religious, because I think about it every day.'

Her mother might have thought it unlikely that her daughter would ever fulfil her ambition, but she could always hope. Reading this letter, she thought the aspiration to be a 'true religious' just one more example of Léonie's oddness, because in that pious household, was not every nun a saint, so what did Léonie mean by it? 'It means I want to be a very good religious and then a saint,' Léonie replied. St Thomas Aquinas could not have put it better! Her family obviously underestimated her understanding; after all, Jesus emphasized that it was not the wise and clever who would enter the kingdom of heaven first, but the 'foolish of this world' and the childlike.

St Francis de Sales had written:

> Let us keep at the feet of our Saviour. Let us practice the small virtues which are fitting for our smallness: patience, kindness to our neighbours, service, humility, gentleness, friendli-

> ness, acceptance of our imperfections. I am not saying that it is not through prayer that we grow; but it must happen slowly, step by step.

This admirably describes Léonie's spiritual journey. Humbly, without a trace of bitterness, envy or jealousy, Léonie accepted that her sisters were better looking, more talented, cleverer than herself, but equally she wanted to give herself to God with all her heart.

After their mother's death, when the other four sisters paired off, Léonie, in the middle, had no-one she could call mother. Always a bit of a loner, later saying that she suffered 'loneliness of heart', she withdrew into her room and into her solitude. Their father did all he could to take their mother's place and ensured that Léonie was not left out. Before his breakdown and the years of his final, painful illness, he took them on various trips and made sure that Léonie was included. Like his young daughter, he, too, was very much drawn to the writings and the example of St Francis de Sales; Thérèse wrote in her autobiography:

> What I noticed especially was the progress he was making in perfection. He had succeeded, like St Francis de Sales, in overcoming his natural impetuosity to such an extent that he appeared to have the most gentle nature in the world.[5]

Léonie's determined attempts to enter the religious life gave her family and the Guérins numerous headaches. Despite her affection for her aunt and the Salesian spirituality, it was not initially to the Visitation sisters that she turned her desires, but to the nearby monastery of Poor Clares. Her mother had often gone there to talk to the sisters of her difficulties and to ask their prayers; she had also made her profession as a Third

Order Franciscan. Léonie sometimes went with her and decided she would like to be a Poor Clare, although her mother wrote, 'When Léonie tells me every day that she will become a Poor Clare nun like those in Alençon I put as much confidence in that as if it were little Thérèse who said it.'

Her first attempt was on 7 October 1886, when the family went to Alençon for a visit. Léonie slipped away and went to the Poor Clare abbey to say she wanted to enter. Strangely, the Abbess advised her to enter immediately, and even supplied her with a habit. This was only a week before Marie entered Carmel on the 15th, throwing everyone into a turmoil. The experiment lasted only two months, because Léonie's fragile health was not up to the austerity of the Poor Clares. She returned to her family 1 December, depressed and in ill health. The New Year, though, provided distractions, with visits to Le Havre in June, where an International Maritime Exhibition was being held. From there, they crossed to Honfleur and visited Notre Dame de Grace, where Léonie prayed that she would be able to fulfil her desires for a religious vocation. It took only a few days, because on 16 July, she entered the Visitation Convent in Caen. This was more suited to her, because its founders, St Francis de Sales and St Jeanne de Chantal, had provided a rule for those whose health could not withstand the rigours of Orders such as the Poor Clares or Carmelites.

Léonie wrote to Thérèse of her happiness: 'I am happy, my dear, in my new family; I am surrounded by affection … how good it seems to me! God has been very kind to me; it is he who led me here, by the hand, and I believe this is where he wants me to be'[6] It was indeed where God wanted her to be, but not yet.

By November, Pauline, now Sister Agnès, was writing to her father from Carmel, 'Léonie is doing better, but we must keep praying for her; it takes so little to make her stumble'. Then, 6 January the following year, she returned home. She occupied her time with housework and visiting her sisters at the Carmel. In her deposition to the tribunal for Thérèse's Cause for canonisation, Léonie noted how loving and generous her little sister was to the poor they met on their walks. Unremarked by the household was Léonie's own heroic charity towards a poor, sick woman whom she nursed and cared for at this time.

Even more difficult for Léonie to bear was to see Thérèse entering Carmel in April that year, fulfilling her yearnings for the religious life, while she herself seemed to be rejected. It is a measure of Léonie's humility and generosity of spirit that she was never jealous or embittered by her sisters' happiness and fulfilment in the religious life. It is notable, though, that in her letters home Thérèse never wrote to Léonie herself, but only added a note at the end to pass on her prayers, saying often that she had 'no time to write further'. Léonie did not receive letters addressed to her personally until she made her third attempt at the religious life later on. Did Thérèse never think that her sister might have appreciated a letter for herself before then?

Their father's illness progressed so rapidly that the following year, 1889, shortly after Thérèse had received the habit, his reason went completely, and for his own safety, in February, the family decided he had to be committed to the asylum at Caen. Céline and Léonie took up lodgings there so as to be near him, and Léonie also had the joy of being near her beloved Visitation convent. After three months their uncle persuaded them to return to Lisieux to live with his family and simply visit their father once a week. Besides those weekly visits, there was more travelling for the two sisters; to the International Exhibition in Paris, to Lourdes, and to Paray-le-Monial for the bicentenary of St Margaret Mary's death, a special occasion for Léonie, who was still pining for the Visitation. As Céline remarked at one point, 'Léonie thinks of nothing but the Visitation; my little affairs don't interest her.'

When M Guérin was left in a bequest a palatial estate at La Musse, the two young girls were often invited to stay there. There were frequent dances and social events. Céline enjoyed them but Léonie did not, lacking the social graces needed for these occasions.

When M Martin's legs became paralysed and there was no danger now of his wandering off, he returned in May to Lisieux. At first he stayed with the Guérins, then in a small rented house with his daughters, which was found nearby, where the burden of nursing was shared with a nurse and a valet.

For Léonie, the turning point came the following month when, instead of joining the rest of the family, including their father, at La Musse, she went to Caen for a retreat at the Visitation. She asked the Prioress if she could try her vocation once again, and with her uncle's consent, she entered on 24 June.

This time, she persevered for three years. To her joy, she was admitted to the Clothing in the habit, 6 April 1894, when she took the name of Sister Thérèse Dosithée, in memory of her aunt. Even the Clothing was a cause of suffering for her, for the tight headdress caused her eczema to flair up, and her head became very itchy. Thérèse now wrote several letters to her, encouraging her on the little way of abandonment to God, humility and love. In one letter, she tells Léonie of an illustration a retreat father had given, of the oak in a crowded forest; hemmed in on all sides, 'The forest oak sees nothing but the heavens; and so all its strength goes to reaching in that direction, and it quickly reaches a great height'. The lesson was that when sufferings crowd, then the only way to look is up.

The year turned into 1895 and Léonie looked forward to her Profession. To her consternation it was decided that she was not ready for it and it was postponed, with no date set. In her distress, Léonie thought of going to another convent at Mans, and when Lent had ended Thérèse, hearing of this, wrote to her, encouraging her by telling her of the delay in her own Profession; of her sadness, and how she coped with it. She recalled thinking, 'What does it matter if I appear poor and destitute of mind and talents? I want to put into practice this counsel from the Imitation: "Let this one take glory in one thing, another in something else, but as for you, set your joy only in contempt of self, in My will and My glory"... When thinking this over, I felt that here was truth and peace!'[7] Thérèse then said she set herself to preparing a dress for Jesus that only he would see, unlike the beautiful dress she had worn for her Clothing. She told Léonie that she should on no account think of going to Mans. She was sure that Léonie did indeed have a Visitation vocation and that it was to be at Caen.

It was not the only time that Thérèse had had a strong sense of Léonie's vocation; even before she herself had entered Carmel she had stated that her family need not worry, because Léonie would enter the Visitation and that she would take her own name and that of St Francis de Sales. At her Profession, as she lay prostrate in Choir as a sign of her surrender, the one prayer Thérèse made was for her sister to become a Visitandine. When Léonie eventually left, 20 July 1895, Thérèse was not discouraged, but told Marie of the Sacred Heart that after her death Léonie would try again and would succeed. Sadly for Léonie, this time the strength needed was not enough. It was not all the fault of her own deficiencies, because the novice mistress was so strict and inflexible that not only Léonie, but other novices also found it too demanding and left at this time.

Léonie returned to Lisieux and lived with the Guérins, still feeling ill at ease with their social gatherings at La Musse, still pining for the Visitation. She made visits to the Carmel, and longed for Thérèse's encouragement and spiritual advice, but became increasingly concerned as 1897 progressed and news of her sister's illness became ever more serious. Thérèse wrote her final note to her 17 July, while Léonie was staying at La Musse:

> The only happiness on earth is to apply oneself to always finding delightful the lot Jesus is giving us. Your lot is so beautiful, dear little sister; if you want to be a saint, this will be easy for you since at the bottom of your heart the world is nothing to you…
>
> You want me to pray in heaven to the Sacred Heart for you. Be sure that I shall not forget to deliver your messages to Him and to ask all that will be necessary for you to become a great saint.

She added, very touchingly, at the bottom of the letter, a postscript that was erased when it was first published: 'I shall write to you at greater length another time; I cannot do so now, for baby has to go to sleep.'[8]

Thérèse was never able to write that longer letter, although she did ask Sister Marie of the Sacred Heart to write one for her, a letter Léonie treasured, with all the others. After her death Thérèse kept her promise to pray for her sister, for at last, 29 January 1899, Léonie entered the Visitation at Caen for another time, and this time it was permanent. A new Mother Superior had realised that the regime in the Novitiate had to be softened, and not only Léonie but some others who had left re-entered and persevered. As the cloister doors closed behind her, Léonie flung herself into her Superior's arms, vowing that the doors would open to her again only when she was carried out in her coffin.

During her Novitiate, Léonie had an indispensable help to guide her in her new life, and that was her sister's autobiography that had just been published. She was deeply moved by what Thérèse had written about her, of the help she had been to her in her sister's earliest years. These pages, which she read over and over again, were the blueprint for her own progress in holiness. Thérèse taught her how to love her weakness and her faults and to make of them the very steps that would lead her to intimate union with God.

Then, at last, she was able to write to her Carmelite sisters that she had been accepted for her Clothing, which would take place 30 June 1899. 'Believe me, there will be rejoicing in Heaven and on earth when you take the habit', Sister Marie of the Sacred Heart wrote to her. 'My little Léonie must become more and more humble, obedient, and loving … even your little Carmelites, for love has wings, and the heart and soul know no distances.'[9]

This letter was only one of many that flew between Carmel and Visitation over the years. With so many of their family now in heaven, those who remained drew ever closer in spirit, and they wanted Léonie, especially, to feel part of the family, however far apart they were in miles. Léonie asked if they could write to her regularly in order to give her spiritual help and advice, and with growing intimacy, was given advice on such mundane things as to how to use tweezers to remove unwanted facial hair!

At her clothing, Léonie did indeed receive the names Thérèse had foretold for her years before—Sister Françoise-Thérèse. Before the ceremony, the Mother Superior said to her, 'Your perseverance in desiring to embrace religious life, and the love you have for our holy vocation, give us hope, my dear sister, that you will joyfully attain the fulfilment of those hopes.' Sister Françoise-Thérèse did not disappoint. She was given various tasks around the convent, working tirelessly and generously at the tasks given her, whether it was in the sacristy—a position she loved—the bursar's office, the refectory or the linen room.

Finally, on 2 July 1900, Feast of the Visitation, the day arrived for which she had longed for so many years, and for which she had striven with undiminished determination, the day of her Profession. It was a day of unmitigated joy, surrounded by the prayers of her Carmelite sisters as well as those of her community. Of the family, only her brother-in-law, Dr François de Néele, Jeanne's husband, was able to attend, because her aunt had died earlier that year and her uncle was ill.

Afterwards she wrote to her Carmelite sisters:

> What a wonderful day! Nothing could distract me from the perfect calm, the heavenly peace which flooded my soul; I have never, never, been so happy! In the evening of that heavenly day, I - like our beloved Thérèse—took off my lovely wreath, to lay it before the Sacred Heart and the most holy Virgin, with no sense of regret; time cannot take away my happiness, for I am the bride of God for all eternity.[10]

When she woke up the morning after her Profession, it was with deep satisfaction that she pressed her Profession crucifix to her heart, saying to herself that no-one could take it away from her, for she now belonged completely to Jesus.

Lacking common sense and proportion, she was never competent enough to be any other than an assistant in any of the offices in which she worked, a fact which hurt her at times, but she was clear-sighted enough to know that she did not have the ability to be in charge, and learnt to accept her limitations. She wrote to Mother Agnès of Jesus, 'I am still doing my humble job in the refectory. Considering how incompetent I am, I should be very honoured to be entrusted with anything in the house... When, sometimes, I catch myself wishing for something more, I quickly submerge myself in the will of God.'[11]

She was very slow in carrying out her tasks, and had a sometimes excessive desire for order that could grate on those quicker and more able than she was. But that very excessive preoccupation with tasks could be put to good use as assistant to the bursar, for instance, a job that gave her more scope than the Refectorian's assistant. 'It is just the job for me,' she wrote to her sisters, telling them of her appointment. 'I put things in order here and there, all through the house. I think of myself as the convent's little donkey.' Nevertheless, she did suffer from the occasional stinging criticisms of her slowness from other sisters, but generously accepting the rebukes in silence and forgiveness.

Her limitations did distress her. 'I have suffered greatly from my inferiority. I have felt keen isolation of heart—of every kind. I experience the same difficulties, again and again: worries, dislikes, weariness of all sorts. But I can feel that all these torments are a purification—that God is at work, and I thank Him for all of it.'[12]

God was indeed using her limitations to bring her to real holiness. Although she thought she was always battling against them and longed to be really humble, in fact others could see that genuine humility, gentleness, and the joy that St Francis de Sales wanted for his daughters, radiated from her. One of the most heart-breaking and poignant things she wrote to her sisters was, 'I believe I am loved, even though I am not at all lovable'. She little realised that her deep humility made her lovable. A visitor to the convent, Mlle Violet Castel, exclaimed to her sister, Sister of Marie of the Trinity at Lisieux Carmel, 'I spend such lovely moments with Sister Françoise-Thérèse during our visits! She might be described as good sense united with the love of God. She is a real little saint—and so humble! She makes everyone love her!'[13] She might lack common sense in doing tasks, but God had given her, without her knowing it, spiritual good sense.

She had never thought that she would see her sisters again, but when, in April 1903, Mother Agnès of Jesus and Mother Marie de Gonzague had to travel to Valognes on business, they took the opportunity to stop at the Visitation. Then, with the Cause of

Thérèse's canonisation progressing, in the April of 1915 she had the great joy of spending a few days at the Lisieux Carmel, to give her eyewitness evidence in the Apostolic Process of her sister's canonisation. For eight wonderful days she had the joy of staying in the Carmel, seeing for herself the places where Thérèse had lived out her life of love and suffering: her cell, the infirmary where she died, the refectory where she, like herself, had been a refectorian. She saw the great Cross in the courtyard where Thérèse had had her photograph taken on her Clothing Day, and which she herself had used for her Clothing card.

By 1915 Françoise-Thérèse accepted that her youngest sister would be raised to the altars, but that had not always been so. After all, she believed, it was only saints renowned for their exceptional penances, miracles and outstanding charisms who were! However much she loved Thérèse and lived by her spirituality, she considered that doing little things humbly for the love of God was not the stuff of which saints were made. When, in 1909, her Superior sought her out in the monastery garden to tell her that canonisation was a definite prospect, Françoise-Thérèse simply continued spreading out the linen, saying without any real emotion, 'Thérèse! She was very kind! But a saint? Really!'

She was invited to be present at the ceremonies of beatification and canonisation, but preferred to remain out of the limelight. Instead, she listened, with her community, to the canonisation ceremony on one of the radio sets sent to Caen and Lisieux on the Pope's orders. In the sermon for the occasion, the Bishop of Bayeux and Lisieux referred to Thérèse's three Carmelite sisters. No mention was made of Léonie. Neither did she seek the limelight when visitors came to Caen hoping to see the sister of the saint. She was helping the portress one day when a visiting priest asked her if he could see St Thérèse's sister. 'We will ask our Mother,' she replied, 'but I don't think that will be possible.'

'Oh, that would be a great disappointment,' the priest replied.

'I can assure you, Father,' Sister Françoise-Thérèse replied with a straight face, 'that you won't miss anything—it isn't worth the trouble.'

The priest left, somewhat shocked and scandalised at such lack of charity. He met the chaplain on his way out, who burst out laughing when told of the conversation. 'My poor Father,' he exclaimed, 'you've been tricked—that was Léonie herself you were talking to!'

Her health had never been strong, but the last eleven years of her life were marked by increasing infirmity. Two attacks of pneumonia severely weakened her and left her permanently stooped. She had trouble with her right knee and had to walk with the aid of a stick. Sister Françoise-Thérèse described herself as 'a little shrivelled old woman'. Knowing that she was mentally slow, her one fear was that she would lose her reason and spend her final years in the asylum, only a short distance away from her convent, where her father had been hospitalised. This trial was not asked of her, though, and she spent her last years surrounded by the love and affectionate care of the Visitation sisters she loved so much. She died 16 June 1941. She, who feared she would never make the grade as a religious, spent forty-three years in the religious life.

Sister Françoise-Thérèse had said that she wanted to be 'a very good religious and then a saint'. Can we doubt that the Lord she loved so much did grant her desire?

Notes

1 Z. and L. Martin, *A Call to a Deeper Love* (New York: St Paul Publications, 2011), translated by Ann Connors Hess, edited by Dr France Renda, p. 7.
2 *Ibid.,* p. 101.
3 M. Baudouin-Croix, *Leonie, a Difficult Life* (Dublin: Veritas Publications, 1993), p. 13.
4 Z. and L. Martin, *A Call to a Deeper Love,* p. 147, note 282.
5 Thérèse of Lisieux, *Story of a Soul* (Washington DC: ICS Publications, 1976), translated by J. Clarke OCD, pp. 152–153
6 *Ibid.,* p. 42.
7 Thérèse of Lisieux, *Letters Vol 11.* (Washington DC: ICS Publications, 1988), translated by J. Clarke OCD, pp. 902-903.
8 *Ibid.,* pp. 1148–1149.
9 Baudouin-Croix, *Leonie,* p. 78.
10 *Ibid.,* p. 83.
11 *Ibid.,* p. 85.
12 *Ibid.,* p. 87.
13 *Ibid.,* p. 88.

4

SISTER GENEVIÈVE OF THE HOLY FACE

CÉLINE MARTIN

Marie and Pauline were more like mothers to Thérèse than sisters. Céline, four years older than her, was the sister closest to her, her playmate and friend. Born in Alençon 28 April, 1869, she was the Martin's seventh child, and was a consolation to her parents after the longed for boy, Joseph Jean, born two years earlier, had tragically died young. Although Céline was strong and robust, as was Thérèse, she suddenly contracted the enteritis that had carried off her two brothers. She had been put into the care of a wet nurse, but her father was so concerned that he would walk up and down in front of the house, until one day he heard Céline crying convulsively. He went into the house and found the baby alone in her crib and no sign of the wet-nurse. He discovered from the neighbours that she was often drunk, and Céline was dying from neglect, so she was immediately brought back home. It was only at the third attempt that a good nurse was found for her, Mme Georges, who lived in the country. With good care and country air, Céline at last began to thrive.

From the very beginning Céline displayed the characteristics that would remain with her throughout her life: headstrong, witty, extremely intelligent, with a genuine sweetness and a deep piety. Her mother wrote that she displayed two tendencies, 'one was a need for life and happiness ... the other, a very tender heart'. Her uncle described her as 'a large-hearted girl'. To her father, she was the intrepid one. Described as a pretty, strapping girl, her robust frame was matched by a like robustness of character. Independent minded, the four-year old Céline declared to her mother one evening, that she didn't like poor people. Her mother, somewhat taken aback, because the children had been brought up to have a great compassion and concern for the poor, said that Jesus wouldn't be happy at that, and wouldn't love her any more.

'I love the good Jesus very much,' Céline replied, 'but I won't love poor people ever in my life. Anyway, I don't want to love them! What does it matter to Jesus? He's definitely the master but I am also the mistress.'

Her mother then realised that Céline was reacting to an incident a few days earlier, when a little girl had mocked her and slapped her in the face on one of their outings. She had been thrown into a rage and refused to accept the indignity for the love of Jesus. However, that night she slept on it and told her mother that she now had a lovely bouquet to give to Jesus and his mother, and that she loved poor people very much now.[1]

When Thérèse was born, the two became inseparable. 'It seemed to me that the same soul animated us', Thérèse wrote, 'that there is between us something so evident and so alike. Always we have been together, our joys, our griefs, all have been shared.' This did not mean that there were no squabbles between them, with Céline, to add a pearl to her crown, letting her take the toys she wanted.

Céline was eight when their mother died, and it affected her as much as it did Thérèse. As Céline herself admitted, she who had been so sweet became an imp of mischief, and in Thérèse's words, 'a naughty little rascal'. Her father enrolled her as a part-time boarder at the Benedictine Abbey, and she soon became head of the class. With her strong character and intelligence she often became quarrelsome, and was, as she said, 'well able to defend myself by the power of a sharp tongue'. In some ways timid—she did not have the courage to present herself for a diploma she had won—in other ways courageous and ready for battle in sticking up for herself and for those she loved, especially her little sister.

As with all the girls, her heart was always at Les Buissonets. This was where the inner life of all the Martin sisters flourished, and despite Céline's absences at school, the bond between her and Thérèse remained as close as ever. However, it underwent a profound change after Thérèse's conversion experience of Christmas 1886. Before then, as Thérèse recounted[2] she often complained that she longed to share Céline's secrets, and would climb on to a stool so as to be as tall as her elder sister, to no avail. Now, her swift maturity meant that the two sisters were able to share their most intimate thoughts. That spiritual closeness flowered in those conversations in the belvedere at Les Buissonets that Thérèse described in her autobiography:

> How sweet were the conversations we held each evening in the belvedere! With enraptured gaze we beheld the white moon rising quietly behind the tall trees, the silvery rays it was casting upon sleeping nature, the bright stars twinkling in the deep skies, the light breath of

> the evening breeze making the snowy clouds float easily along; all this raised our souls to heaven, that beautiful heaven whose obverse side alone we were able to contemplate.
>
> It was in this way He deigned to manifest Himself in our souls, but how light and transparent the veil was which hid Jesus from our gaze! Doubt was impossible, and faith and hope were unnecessary, and *Love* made us find on earth the One whom we were seeking.[3]

For Thérèse this was definitely not mere nineteenth century sentimentality, and it was equally true for Céline who, from her heart, could echo Teresa of Avila's cry: 'I want to see God'. Early on, she had declared that she wanted to be a religious. These times of intense fervour were as deep and true for Céline as they were for Thérèse, for they gave her the strength not only to confront but also embrace the heartaches and upheavals that fell upon the family in quick succession in the years to come.

Céline was thirteen when Pauline entered Carmel. Four years later, in 1886, when she was seventeen, and Léonie had entered the Visitation Order for another attempt at the religious life, followed shortly by Marie's entrance into the same Carmel as Pauline, Marie considered that Céline was mature enough to take up the reins of looking after the depleted household. When, the following year, Thérèse expressed her determination to enter Carmel as well, Céline put aside for the time being her own long-cherished desire for the religious life.

After Thérèse had entered Carmel, it fell to Céline to nurse their father through his distressing illness until his death six years later. At first, he was looked after at home, but when his symptoms became too distressing and dangerous to himself, with great reluctance in the February of 1889 Céline was persuaded to allow him to be looked after at the Bon Sauveur asylum in Caen. For the first few months she and Léonie stayed with him at Caen until, at their uncle's insistence, they returned in May to Lisieux. Like Thérèse, Céline could see in their father's illness, which he himself accepted lovingly from the hand of God, God's purifying love for them and wrote to her sisters in Carmel:

> Little sisters, I want to be happy in our tribulations and to do even more: to thank God for the bitterness of our humiliations. I do not know why, but instead of receiving these trials with bitterness and complaint, I see something mysterious and divine in the conduct of our Lord towards us! Besides, did he himself not pass through all humiliations?… I admit that the opinion of others means nothing to me.
>
> Ah! If you knew how I see the finger of God in all our trials! Yes, everything in them bears the visible imprint of his divine finger.[4]

Céline's remark about the opinions of others was prompted by the gossip in the town, that felt that M Martin's illness was in large part caused by so many of his daughters leaving him for the religious life.

On Christmas Day 1889, the lease on Les Buissonets came to an end and the decision was made for Céline and Léonie to move in permanently with the Guérin family; M Guérin had recently been left a substantial legacy which enabled him to retire from his pharmaceutical practice and move in to a magnificent mansion on the rue Paul Banaston, as well as the country mansion at La Musse. It was with great sadness that Céline oversaw the removal of their precious possessions, some of which went to the Carmel, and picked a last ivy leaf to remind her of the happy times they had spent in their beloved home.

When, in May 1892, M Martin became paralysed in his legs and there was no danger of him wandering off, it was felt safe for him to return to Lisieux, where Céline nursed him devotedly until his death. This was also a time of great flowering for her. She had exceptional artistic talents, and her uncle arranged for her to have lessons from M Krug, a well-known local artist. With her enquiring mind and thirst for learning, she read the works of Plato and scientific journals, the classics and the Scriptures. For her own benefit, she copied out numerous passages from the Scriptures, which were to be of great benefit to Thérèse as she in her turn discovered the riches of the Scriptures, but without possessing a complete Bible of her own.

Céline was also very practical and was able, for example, to take apart a sewing machine, memorise all the parts and put it back together again. She also discovered photography, and soon immersed herself in the new hobby, which she was able to take with her into Carmel and which gave the world the numerous photos we have of Thérèse and the community.

She and Léonie were frequent guests of the Guérins, both at their house in Lisieux and at La Musse. The luxury of La Musse disturbed her, though, when she compared it with the poverty of the villagers they visited, and also with the derelict church nearby where the Blessed Sacrament was kept, and which the family helped restore. It was also difficult for her to retain her times for quietness and for prayer amid the social whirl, the parties, dances and soirées. These had an additional danger because, although she wasn't beautiful in a conventional sense, her vitality, intelligence and charm meant that she had numerous offers of marriage, some of which were very tempting. In Carmel, Thérèse was terrified that her sister would be drawn away from her vocation and the community where she longed for her sister to be, and she intensified her prayers for her. The result was that, at one dance, Céline and her partner found themselves unable to move, and both of them had to sit down in some confusion.

Fr Pichon also put a new temptation in her way. Aware of her talents and her gift for organisation, he was keen for her to join him in Canada where he was hoping to found a religious order, with Céline as foundress, to help him in his apostolic work there. Céline also met with great opposition from her aunt and uncle, as well as from Canon Delatroëtte, ecclesiastical Superior to the Carmel, who had earlier opposed Thérèse's entry. He was sympathetic to Céline, but felt, with some justification, that to have a fourth blood sister in the community would be against the spirit and the letter of the Rule.

During this time, though, Thérèse in Carmel was growing ever more certain in her spiritual maturity and the letters that passed between the two were a great help in keeping Céline true to her desire to follow her sister into Carmel. Thérèse told her sister later that she had never cried so much in all her life at the thought that Céline might not be permitted to enter. However, despite all these obstacles, finally, on 14 September, Feast of the Exaltation of the Holy Cross, six weeks after their father's death, she joined her three sisters in Carmel.

Now at last in Carmel, Céline sat down on the straw-filled mattress on her bed in the quietness of her cell, exhausted with the events of the past few days: the last-minute nerves and doubts that beset her before she stepped over the threshold of Carmel; embracing her three sisters as the enclosure door closed behind her, and seeing the smiling face of Thérèse, who had been appointed as her angel. She had taken Céline, now Sister Marie of the Holy Face, to her cell and showed her a poem, written in her father's hand, that Thérèse had pinned to the pillow on the bed. Seeing it, the tears she had not shed during the previous months and years, now flowed down her cheeks.

For now, she savoured the first few minutes of her first few steps in Carmel. Adapting was not easy; she found the hardness of her bed difficult to get used to at first, and her back ached when holding the heavy Office book in Choir. It took her a year to get used to the Carmelite diet, rich in carbohydrates. But it was the inner battles that she found most surprising and disturbing. She had been used to running her own household and overseeing all her father's affairs, and now, as the youngest, she had to be at the beck and call of everyone, with every decision made for her. She had been admired for her inner strength that had taken her through those challenging times. Now, to her surprise, it was the small things of religious life that she found hardest to deal with. As she wrote later:

> That there should be interior struggles in the religious life might come as a surprise to many readers. I confess that at the beginning of my Carmelite life I also experienced some astonishment at this very thing. To me it seemed that, having made the supreme sacrifice of complete

> separation from loved ones, and utter renunciation of the world, it should have been relatively easy to bear the thousand and one crosses of community life. My own petty reactions, however, to the personal trials that came my way shortly after my entrance disabused me of this false notion.[5]

Céline, like everyone who enters religious life, brought into it her own character and personality. Her independence of thought had to bend before the restrictions of the Rule. She tackled all the tasks she was given with a zeal that wanted everything done with utmost perfection, and although this was laudable, Thérèse had to help her become more detached from the task in hand, where pride could lurk at the satisfaction she gained at a task well done. She found it irksome to stop doing something she was engrossed in at the first stroke of the bell. Nevertheless, this was the life she wanted and which she embraced with all her heart.

Céline was accepted for her Clothing, which would take place 5 February 1895. Before that, though, she was very upset when her superiors decided that she should change her name to that of the saintly foundress who had died four years previously, Geneviève of St Teresa. Coming out of recreation that evening when the decision was ratified, Céline found a note that Thérèse had hastily written in pencil, in her pocket. It was her new name, 'Sister Geneviève of Saint Teresa—little Thérèse is the first to write it!'

The very deep bond that had united the two sisters at home persisted in Carmel, although there were strains, because, however much Geneviève appreciated her younger sister, that younger sister was now her teacher and mentor, and older than her in the religious life. After her Profession 24 February the following year, at the hands of her sister, Mother Agnès of Jesus, and the re-election of Mother Marie de Gonzague shortly afterwards, Thérèse was formally appointed as assistant Novice Mistress and she had more authority over the novices under her care.

Thérèse was keen to teach them her Little Way of spiritual childhood and complete abandonment to the merciful love of God. Her sister was the first one who made with her the Act of Oblation to Merciful Love, and Geneviève later wrote: 'I am the first one to have followed her little way. She opened the door, and I dashed in after her',[6] but in fact she did not accept it without question. The queries and objections both she and the other novices had, meant that Thérèse had to think through her teaching, illustrating it with stories, parables and examples, expressing it in different ways suited to their different temperaments. One day, Geneviève, recognising how far more advanced her sister was in union with God and how her own many faults kept recurring, sighed that she would never get on top of them. 'Then go beneath them', was the reply. Thérèse reminded her of the story she had told, when one day the doctor's horse had been blocking the way into the house; the adults were unable to go round it, but little Thérèse simply slipped under it.

Thérèse encouraged the novices to speak frankly and even critically of her, and they did not hesitate to do so. She was being appreciated by more of the community, though by no means all of them, and she said that she preferred vinegar to sugar, preferring to hear something other than praises. She wrote that when her soul was 'tired of too sweet a nourishment, and Jesus permits someone to serve it a good little salad, well seasoned with vinegar and spices, nothing is missing except the oil which gives it added flavour.'[7] She added that 'this good little salad is served up to me by the novices at a time I least expect it', and this reflection was inspired by an occasion when the 'salad' was served up by none other than Sister Geneviève.

By now, Thérèse was becoming seriously ill, and Geneviève was appointed assistant infirmarian so that she could be with her sister more often. When Thérèse was moved down to the infirmary Geneviève was given a room next to her sister, so that she could be on call day and night. This was not an unmixed blessing for her, because she also had to look after another sister in the infirmary, the elderly Mother Hérmance of the Heart of Jesus, who, because of her difficult character, was a great trial to the infirmarians. Geneviève admitted to her sister that when the strain of being called on at every opportunity to perform some trifling service became too great, she would run crouched beneath the infirmary window so that the old sister wouldn't see her. Thérèse, who would have loved to have been infirmarian, responded that she would have deliberately gone past the sister's room in order to be called on; this was not an idle response, because this is what she had done to other sisters when working for them. Perhaps this was no consolation to Geneviève as she compared her sister's heroic love to her failure in love!

Knowing how hard her death would be to her beloved sister, Thérèse was unfailingly cheerful, despite her atrocious suffering. One day Geneviève said to her, 'You will look down on us from on high, won't you?'

'No, I will come down,' Thérèse replied, and her sister was later able to experience the truth of this promise. During her last agony, as Geneviève was moistening her sister's parched lips, Thérèse looked at her 'with a prophetic insistence. Her look was filled with tenderness and at the same time a supernatural expression of encouragement and promise, as if to say "Go, go, my Céline! I will be with you" '[8]

As Thérèse uttered her final words, 'My God, I love you', Geneviève left the infirmary, her heart ready to break with grief. Outside, the sky was heavy and leaden, the stars obscured by the rain. Sobbing, Geneviève said, 'If only there were stars in the heavens!' The sky suddenly became serene, the rain stopped and the stars broke through. She took this as an assurance of her sister's continuing presence, an assurance which would return to her in the days ahead.

With the publication of Thérèse's autobiography some three years later, Geneviève became immersed in work promoting her sister's cause for beatification and canonisation, responding to the thousands of requests for pictures, relics and reminiscences. Although she had taken many photos of Thérèse, Geneviève felt that they did not capture her essence, so it was her portraits that were included in subsequent editions and the holy pictures sent out by the monastery. It is true that because of the primitive nature of early photography, subjects had to remain still for several seconds, which made them look rather wooden. Because it was not considered proper for them to smile, none of the photos capture Thérèse's radiant smile, so we do not see that side of her nature in the photos.

Geneviève soon wrote a short account of her sister's life and also reminiscences of the teaching she received as her novice. Then, as Thérèse's Cause progressed, her talent for organisation came into play and she was indispensable in building up the archives of all the material, the letters, the reminiscences and also the accounts of miracles that were received at the monastery. Eventually, a central bureau was set up to co-ordinate everything.

However busy she was, Geneviève was meticulous in following all the community observances, but remarked wryly that as she climbed the stairs to her cell and seeing a cartouche on the wall, 'Today a little work! Tomorrow, eternal rest!' changed it in her mind to 'Much work today! And after a long time, alas! eternal rest!'

Did this mean that after all Thérèse's teaching about not being absorbed in work Geneviève had slipped back to her old habits? Is it not, rather, an illustration of how her Little Way could be manifested in various ways according to a person's different temperament? Geneviève lived out the Little Way and expressed her love for God by using the particular gifts he had given her. She used her lively intellect and great capacity for hard work, her scholar's mind, in God's service. She eventually had access to copies of the full Bible in different translations, which, like Thérèse, she loved to study minutely. Like Thérèse, she would have loved to study Greek, Hebrew and even Aramaic, in order to understand the Scriptures at source. She collected photos and maps of the Holy Land and made copious and meticulous notes on the Scriptures which were worthy of a scholar.

Thérèse said that learned books made her head ache and that the Gospels were enough to give her food for prayer, but Geneviève had a different mind and different needs. For her, everything was material that fed her passion for the person of Christ, who was the focus of everything in her life. It was a question of reaching the same goal of union with Christ as her sister's, but by a different path. To live in his presence, as she did, was her unique vocation, expressed in her own way.

The focus of her love for Christ was typified in the Holy Face. In Thérèse's time this was the image of the Holy Face promulgated by the holy man of Tours, M Dupont, based on Veronica's veil, but on 10 November 1897, a letter from the king of Italy authorised the distribution of the photos taken of the Holy Shroud of Turin, including the negatives. M Guérin obtained a copy, which he passed on to his niece. Geneviève gazed on it in tears; much as she appreciated the Tours image, it didn't portray the Christ she envisaged, but this did. The following Easter, she started work on a grisaille of the Holy Face, using a life size photo, but even then she used a magnifying glass to capture the smallest detail. In 1909, the resulting painting won the grand prize at the International Exposition of Religious Art in Holland, and reproductions were distributed in their thousands. The Pope sent her a medal in appreciation of her work, and this delighted her more than any secular award. On 14 November 1914, Mother Agnès of Jesus gave her permission to add 'of the Holy Face' to her name, which she placed before that 'of St Teresa'.

She also had a deep love of the Mother of Christ, and, like Thérèse, was impatient of those who would put her on an impossible pedestal. She wrote on 9 October 1935, of an experience she had had the previous evening, which sums up her relationship with Mary:

> [D]uring the time of silence, I felt ineffably united to my heavenly Mother; I experienced an indefinable feeling I dare not express. It

> seemed to me that the Blessed Virgin was here with us, that she was my sister, my friend; there was a familiarity between us, a kind of equality like that of a family. Oh, how pleasant it was![9]

This was completely in the Carmelite tradition, where Mary is seen, not only as Queen and Mother, but also as sister, ever since the first friars named themselves as the 'Brothers of Our Lady of Mount Carmel'.

Geneviève showed the same independence of thought when she was called to give evidence at the tribunals set up to examine the heroic nature of her sister's life. When asked what her motive was for seeking Thérèse's canonisation, she replied that it was solely to advance the Little Way of Spiritual Childhood. She described the reaction of the tribunal to this:

> Then they took fright, and every time I spoke those words 'Little Way', they gave a start, and the Promoter of the Faith, M Dubosq, said to me, 'If you speak of a "Way", you will defeat the Cause; you know very well that the Cause of Mother Chapuis was abandoned for that reason.'[10]

'Too bad', was Geneviève's response; she had to tell the truth, whatever the outcome and however inconvenient. In the event, she was vindicated when Pope Benedict XV, in his homily for Thérèse's beatification, made specific reference to the Little Way.

It could be said that spiritual childhood found in her character unlikely ground. Geneviève saw her life as an example that the Little Way of Spiritual Childhood could be lived by anyone. If we had only Thérèse as an example it would be easy to become discouraged by the swiftness with which she reached a high degree of sanctity; in Céline's words, 'With Thérèse, the "bomb" of graces exploded on the spot!' In God's designs, as with most, Geneviève's virtues and the graces given to her would mature throughout her long life.

As the passage quoted above makes clear, she was conscious throughout her life of her temperament against which she had to battle to the end. When, after Thérèse's death, she became the monastery's archivist, she would regret the sharp word spoken if someone interrupted her at work, her moods and her 'outbursts'. This was the flip-side of the positive virtues of a quick mind and a humorous tongue, and the ground of her genuine humility, a humility based on her only too clear realisation of her faults. Thérèse said that she came to Jesus with empty hands. Céline said that her long life was drawing to a close on a pile of zeros. 'I prefer to be clothed solely with the works of Jesus and for my heavenly Father to judge me according to them.' That pile of zeros was true spiritual childhood. One of the sisters wrote of her towards the end of her life:

> Happy, lucid, courageous, interested in everything, eager for details and explanations … about everything just as much as about heaven, her beautiful smile, her patience in suffering show to what point authentic spiritual childhood inspires her. She has a radiance of youth about her that does good to those who approach her … she witnesses by her own life at a time when one does not put on an act. Everything about her, moreover, is simple and spontaneous.[11]

When Thérèse was beatified in 1923 and canonised in 1925, this added to Geneviève's burden of work. She proved an indispensable aide to Mother Agnès, helping with the volume of correspondence, writing her own account of Thérèse's life, not to mention all her painting. In 1927 the possibility of building a basilica was raised, and Geneviève discovered another talent, for deciphering architects' plans, not only for the basilica, but also for necessary changes to the monastery and for accommodation for the increasing numbers of pilgrims. She was relieved of all duties within the monastery so that she could devote herself to the work connected with Thérèse.

She played an indispensable part in community life, but like Thérèse she could not be admitted to the Chapter and take part in the decision-making of the community, because the rules said that only two sisters of the same family could be admitted. This changed in 1915, when the Carmelite Superior General intervened and granted her the necessary permission. In 1929, she was made a Council Sister, an office she held until her death.

During the First World War the community had shared in the general hardships of the country at that time. It was different at the outbreak of the Second World War, the main difference being the number of soldiers who found their way to Lisieux and from there spread devotion to Thérèse. When the community took refuge in the crypt of the Basilica Geneviève had to leave behind all the precious relics and archives of her sister that she had so lovingly amassed, but she was calm and at peace, saying to the sister who was with her, 'If our whole monastery disappeared, the spirit would still remain'. What preoccupied her more was the fact that for the first time in forty years she was meeting other people without her veil down, and she hated being the object of curiosity and even veneration as being the sister of the saint, just as she had hated having to go to the parlour to meet various dignitaries.

The War years brought sadness of a personal nature when both Marie of the Sacred Heart and then Léonie, died. Now there were just the two sisters left, and they became even closer. She herself longed for heaven, but she had more years yet to wait.

On 24 February 1946, Geneviève celebrated the Golden Jubilee of her Profession; she was seventy-eight years old. The Apostolic Nuncio, Mgr Roncalli, the future Pope John XX111, presided at the celebration Mass. Meeting him in the cloister afterwards, Geneviève told him that he would be the next Pope. Mgr Roncalli said that he would prefer to know that he would go to heaven. 'Leave that to God,' was her reply, 'but you will be Pope.'

Looking back over the years, Geneviève could see only too clearly her faults, but also the Lord's unfailing love. 'I feel that I am queen of the Imperfect,' she would say. 'My kingdom is extremely vast, and I have myriads of subjects but, whatever they do, they cannot surpass their queen on this,'[12] recalling Thérèse saying to her, 'It is enough to humble oneself, to bear one's imperfections with gentleness'.

In 1951 Mother Agnès of Jesus died in her ninetieth year, leaving Geneviève as the sole survivor of the five sisters. She herself was eighty-two. 'I notice very little here below,' she wrote now. 'My heart and my thoughts are truly in heaven without any sensible consolation. It is a strong and deep feeling. I am always talking to my "Little Mother"', as she called Mother Agnès. 'We two old women were fused together in these last years.'[13]

Geneviève had many health problems by now, but it did not stop her activity. From 1900 onwards she suffered from crippling arthritis in her knees, which eventually spread right through her body. In 1942 she developed sciatica and gout, plus other pulmonary and stomach complications. What was even harder for her was loss of hearing and eyesight, which was doubly difficult with someone who was so interested in whatever was going on around her, and who still retained her enquiring mind and sharp intellect. She still savoured her reading, which included not only the latest in theology, but also discoveries in the secular world that revealed more of the world that God had created. For her, there was no dichotomy between her faith and what science discovered. She wrote:

> He is a Father to me, and I love him unto folly, passionately … My only desire is to know him more and more, to attain to the ultimate limits of this knowledge on earth, and later in heaven … and to that, I feel it is necessary to attain the ultimate limits of humility; which is why I keep begging for it so insistently. That sums up the whole of my poor soul.[14]

This also sums up her character—her fiery yet childlike love of God, her insatiable thirst for knowledge and understanding, realising that the more we can come to both heart- and head- knowledge of him here on earth, the greater will be our union with him in heaven. Above all, her search for humility, which she surely received without realising it, was manifested in her unique character of boldness, courage and intelligence.

Despite her age and difficulties in walking and seeing, she still continued to write, especially to combat derogatory remarks that were being made about her father and her family. Nevertheless, the cause for the beatification and canonisation of both her parents had begun, and she was called to give evidence. This meant more writing for her, and despite her infirmities, she could be seen climbing up to the attic to check the archives for a reference, a date, an anecdote, still with her meticulous scholar's mind.

She was fast approaching that 'death of his saints' that she had witnessed in the four sisters who had gone before her, and which she longed for for herself. The pain and suffering of her last days were a true calvary; on 24 February 1959, the anniversary of her Profession, she received communion for the last time, and all knew the end was near. The following day, her suffering eased a little, and her Prioress confirmed that today would be the day when she would meet her Lord face to face. 'Yes, you are struggling, it is a hard fight! But you will have the victory because Jesus is with you.' Geneviève repeated this triumphal note as she said her last word, 'Jesus!' She suddenly looked up, her eyes luminous and with such a sense of elation that even the doctor knelt down in prayer. This lasted for perhaps ten minutes before she quietly slipped away, her face relaxing into a beautiful majesty.

Shortly before her death, Geneviève's Prioress remarked that the fruits of spiritual childhood were evident in her. In reply Geneviève said:

> Perhaps little Thérèse wants to show in her Céline that one can remain little and simple even in extreme old age. But one must always say: 'It is, you, Lord, who have accomplished all our works.' Yes, it is he alone, for I could well be caught up in the temptation to sadness as well as fear. It is true that I have no fear at all, none at all, of God. Oh! I am going to be so happy to see him, to see his Humanity! I have desired him so much! Yet, I have much offended him; but, even so, I am very sure that Jesus will say to me as to the woman in the Gospel: 'Go, my daughter, your sins are forgiven'[15].

Time and time again Geneviève mentions the peace of heart she enjoyed, despite her struggles: 'Despite the often very sharp trials that have marked my path,' she wrote at the time of her Golden Jubilee, 'I find, in the end, that Our Lord has not failed in his promise and that "in leaving all things" I have found not only "the hundredfold", but I went further, to "the thousand-fold", in joy and interior peace.'

'Oh! I am going to be so happy to see him, to see his Humanity!' Throughout her life it was the humanity of Jesus that was her polestar, and above all the human face of Jesus. 'My devotion to the Holy Face,' she said, 'is the summary of my devotion to the Sacred Humanity of Jesus.'

'It is you, Lord, who have accomplished all our works.' This verse from Scripture summed up for Geneviève her spirituality and it lies at the heart of Thérèse's teaching on spiritual childhood. Geneviève expressed it in another way in the motto she adopted as her own: 'The one who loses wins.' She felt that she never succeeded in overcoming her faults of character and temperament, but she used this as her greatest weapon to win the heart of Jesus. What she could not do herself, Jesus could do and did do, as her peace of soul testified.

Notes

1 Z. and L. Martin, *A Call to a Deeper Love* (New York: St Paul Publications, 2011), translated by Ann Connors Hess, edited by Dr France Renda, pp. 131-132.

2 Thérèse of Lisieux, *Story of a Soul* (Washington DC: ICS Publications, 1976), translated by J. Clarke OCD, p. 103.

3 *Ibid.,* pp. 103-104.

4 S.-J. Piat, OFM, *Céline, Sister Geneviève of the Holy Face* (San Francisco: Ignatius Press, 1977), pp. 40–41.

5 C. Martin, (Sister Geneviève of the Holy Face), *My Sister Saint Thérèse* (Rockford, Illinois: Tan Books, 1959), p. 10.

6 Piat, *Céline,* p. 107.

7 Thérèse of Lisieux, *Story of a Soul,* p. 244.

8 Piat, *Céline,* p. 90.

9 *Ibid.,* p. 107.

10 *Ibid.,* p. 110.

11 *Ibid.,* p. 180.

12 *Ibid.,* p. 133.

13 *Ibid.,* p. 137.

14 *Ibid.,* pp. 161–162.

15 *Ibid.,* p. 181.

5

MOTHER GENEVIÈVE OF ST TERESA

FOUNDRESS

IT WAS SAID of Cardinal Pole, who at the time of the Reformation barely escaped being elected as the only English Pope after Adrian IV, that he would have made a *good* Pope but not a good *Pope.* Someone may be a very saintly person, but that does not necessarily fit them for high office. The same might be said of Mother Geneviève of St Teresa, who was one of the founding sisters of the Lisieux Carmel.

Mother Geneviève was still living when Thérèse entered the community, the only surviving sister of the original community. As Clare Marie Radegunda Bertrand, she was born in Poitiers 1805, the eldest daughter with two younger brothers. The family was comfortably off, with a strong religious faith. She was a precocious child, able to read at the age of three and a half, and preferred reading to more boisterous games. The parish priest, Fr de Beauregard, who later became Bishop of Orléans, recognised the young girl as especially spiritually gifted, and prepared her for her First Communion with great care. As he wrote to her some twenty years later, 'From your earliest years I saw in you the makings of a saint.'

The family circumstances changed when Clare was sixteen and her mother died, leaving her to become the much-loved mother to her younger brothers. To add to their problems, her father, who was a business agent, found himself in such severe financial difficulties that they might have had to sell their home. One evening, when her father went out to arrange a sale, Clare went to her room, overcome with the weight of the burden thrust upon her and of fear for the future for their family. Her eyes fell on a picture of Our Lord, which suddenly grew luminous, and at the same time she was flooded with light. Without words, the Lord gave her to understand the value of suffering and the nothingness of the material world. Her tears turned now to gratitude and joy, and she felt ready to face whatever trials would come their way. However, the Lord did not want the sacrifice of losing the family home, because a cousin gave them the funds they needed to keep it, and their father was assured of the post he wanted.

A year later, and Clare was praying to discover God's will for her. As she described it:

> I was alone in my room; I had knelt down to make my morning prayer when suddenly the room seemed to disappear; I no longer knew where I was, or whether or not I had a body. I seemed to be surrounded by a wonderful light, and my soul was flooded with ineffable joy. Then I heard a voice so melodious that no earthly music can compare with it, and it sang these words, leaving a mysterious interval between them: 'To be the spouse of God—what an honour is this! What a privilege!'[1]

Everything then returned to normal. The word 'Carmel' had not been spoken, but Clare understood that that was where she was called to be. However, her father had some inkling of where her heart was turning, because, when Fr de Beauregard became bishop of Orléans, shortly after she took as her confessor and spiritual director the chaplain to the Carmel, Fr de Rochemonteix. He went to see the Prioress and obtained from her the assurance that she would not be allowed to enter, for he needed his daughter so much at home. When Clare went to see the Prioress, Mother Aimée of Jesus, she replied: 'You want to make a vow of obedience, do you not, my child? Very well, you are going to practice it now by going home to your father. I will let you know when you may enter.'

It was a great disappointment, but because she took it as God's will for her, it filled Clare with a deep peace. She understood that she could not enter while her father was living. She continued to look after her family, dearly loved for her gentleness and goodness. She was described as being 'naturally gentle, kind and refined. In spite of a somewhat cold manner her nature was ardent, and she possessed a loving and generous heart, a lively intelligence, and great common sense, joined with a childlike simplicity.'[2] Not surprisingly, she received many offers of marriage, and she was received by the upper echelons of polite society, even though her family's standing was now modest.

Then, when she was twenty four, her father died and she was free to follow her vocation into Carmel. However, to test her, Fr de Rochemonteix pretended not to believe in her vocation, but lifted his objections as the new year of 1830 began. She entered Carmel 26 March 1830 and was given the name of Geneviève of St Teresa. Mother Aimée of Jesus greeted her with the words: 'My child, if you want to be holy and always happy, remember this—never let anyone know who pleases or displeases you, whom you find agreeable or disagreeable, what you like or dislike.' It was a programme she adopted as her own. The only thing that marred her happiness in her new life during her period as a postulant was the humiliation that the manual work which came so easily to her at home now deserted her and she found herself incapable of the easiest of sewing tasks.

She was clothed with the habit and her period as a novice began joyfully. However, six months before her Profession, Fr de Rochemonteix preached a retreat, during which he described the three states in which a soul in a state of grace might find itself. Sister Geneviève recognised herself in none of them, and it left her in a state of terror. After Matins she went back to her cell, unable to pray. 'I sat down on my bed', she recounted later, 'when all at once, in the silence of the night, a strange voice, which seemed to come from without, said to me, loudly and distinctly: "You could have done it, and yet you would not!"'

This was evidently not an interior locution from God, which she fairly frequently received, but from the devil, because it left her still in agony of soul, not in the peace a locution from God would have brought. She seized her crucifix and held it in the direction of the voice, saying, 'My God, forgive me! Forgive me! Here is my pledge!' feeling that she was damned. In the morning she went to Confession as soon as possible, and received as her penance a novena of communions. She approached the altar feeling as if she was committing a sacrilege, but as she received the Sacred Host her peace returned and all she could feel for her sins was a deep and loving contrition.

Geneviève was Professed 22 July 1831 in great dryness of spirit, which did not lift for some time. Feeling that God had rejected her self-offering, she asked her Prioress to give her some work that would help her sisters. She was made third infirmarian, and nursed devotedly, day and night, a sister who was covered with open and putrefying sores. On the evening of the sister's death, the doctor remarked that 'the Sister who nursed this nun must be a saint, for without a special aid from God it would not have been possible for anyone to have stood for so long such a tainted atmosphere.'

There was much for her to do in the infirmary, for many of the sisters were elderly, having lived through the horrors of the French Revolution, the Napoleonic wars and the attacks against religion, then the upheavals of the restoration of the monarchy. Even now, despite a certain resurgence of faith, there was still in France great antagonism against the Church.

Gradually her sense of union with God became stronger, and the only sadness came when her beloved Prioress, Mother Aimée of Jesus, died. Mother Pauline was elected Prioress, and a little while afterwards Geneviève was made Provisor; being in charge of providing the meals for the community and overseeing the kitchen gave her the opportunity to lavish her love and concern on any sister who needed extra care.

Unknown to her, plans were afoot to make a new foundation, and in preparation for this she was appointed Novice Mistress in 1837. The Lord had warned her in a locution the evening before that this would happen, and so in all humility she accepted this important role of forming young souls in the Carmelite way of life. When plans for the new foundation at Lisieux were finalised she was also named Subprioress, with Sister Elizabeth of St Louis as Prioress. There was a deep bond between the two of them, which was necessary for the trials and hardships they would face together.

The little group of two professed sisters and four novices arrived at their new home on the Chaussée de Beuvilliers 16 March 1838. Despite the possibility of attack by anti-Catholics, they travelled in their habits, the two professed in their long black veils, and arrived at the poor little house at night in driving rain. It was a temporary arrangement, being part of the house of a benefactor, Mme Le Boucher, and drew comparison with the little stable at Bethlehem, or of the first foundations of St Teresa of Avila. The straw-roofed dwelling was by the river and so cramped that they had to use much ingenuity in making it even remotely resembling a monastery. One room, only eighteen feet square, was partitioned off into three sections; one section was the kitchen, the second was a refectory and recreation room, the third was the Subprioress's cell. She had to step carefully when leaving her cell in order not to upset the stove or tread on dishes. The dishes were especially precious because there were so few of them; at meal times they had to be washed up after the first course in order to serve for the dessert—that is, when they had that much to eat.

Within five months a new property was found on the Rue de Livarot, and on 14 August, which, providentially, was the day the first monastery of the Teresian Reform had been established, the Bishop came to bless it. Because building works were still in progress, the nuns eventually moved in 5 September 1838. Even this was only a marginal improvement over their previous house. The loft was portioned off for cells, and the kitchen and refectory had to be put on the second floor, which made it a hard chore for the lay sisters to carry water buckets, for example, up the flights of stairs. However, Mother Elizabeth proved to have great powers of organisation as the little community settled in and new postulants were admitted. Sadly, after only three and a half years in office she died, and Mother Geneviève was elected Prioress. In all, she was elected Prioress for five terms of office, and so oversaw much of the community's growth and development. Over the years houses on either side were bought and extensions added when they had funds to do so. Extra cells and the infirmary wing had been built only ten years before Thérèse entered, and new parlours were added during her time there, when she had to tell her relatives that for a short while they could not visit.

Mother Geneviève's first term in office was a very difficult one. Their chaplain, Fr Sauvage, was in favour of her election, but after she had been installed, he opened a letter that had been sent to him from Mother Pauline in Poitiers. The letter, which was found among his papers after his death, said: 'Do not name Geneviève as Prioress, for she is not capable of filling such a difficult office'. He therefore refused to let the Prioress make the slightest decision without his authorisation and lost all confidence in her. Nevertheless, the community thought differently, and she was elected unanimously for a second term. Fr Sauvage had another concern, because Mother Elizabeth and Mother Geneviève had been loaned to the Lisieux foundation for only three years. When, in 1849, a year after leaving her second term of office, an internal tumour first appeared, and from which she was to suffer for the rest of her life, the Poitiers Carmel wanted her back to nurse her, but Fr Sauvage managed to have the conditions changed so that Mother Geneviève was given definitively to the Lisieux Carmel.

When the little band had first left for Lisieux, Bishop de Beauregard had sent her on her way with the words, 'You are going to Lisieux, not to build of material stones, but to raise in God's honour an edifice of living stones, of souls who are vowed to Him.' In many ways Mother Geneviève had all the qualities that her daughter Thérèse most admired and strove for in her own life. She had a maternal kindness, she was tender and self-sacrificing, meticulous about the care of sick sisters and with heroic self-contempt for her own sufferings; she had an intense interior life and a childlike humility.

Having guided the community for fifteen years those qualities should have led to a community that was inspired by those virtues to have a like fervour, but in many ways this was not so. In the letter Mother Pauline had sent to Fr Sauvage, she might have seen in Mother Geneviève the downside of those very qualities; that she had too great a leniency and was not a strong, natural and influential leader, the qualities needed to establish a young and developing community. When Thérèse entered, there were many sisters who perhaps had no real vocation to the religious life; there were few who had the intellectual and religious training to appreciate the rich Carmelite heritage which was the milieu into which they had entered. Some of these would have been accepted into the community under the leadership of Mother Geneviève. To some extent, that was not her fault, for there was a tendency then for families to send their unmarriageable or superfluous girls to convents, whether they had a vocation or no, but it did tend to make problems for the communities who received them.

Not being a strong leader, she was overshadowed by the entry into the Carmel in 1860 of Marie-Adele-Rosalie de Virville who took the name of Marie de Gonzague. Mother Geneviève had come through her trial of the justice of God but Marie de Gonzague was strongly drawn to mortifications and austerities beyond those laid down by the Carmelite Rule. After she had been elected to her first term as Prioress she instilled this approach into the community, and Mother Geneviève had to warn her, trying to encourage her to follow her own more balanced approach:

> Be careful, for without great prudence and discernment they can lead to vanity and pride and can feed self-love. Teach your daughters to break their wills, to practise charity, to fulfil perfectly all the Rule. There lies true penance which is always pleasing to God.[3]

Such counsel admirably sums up the way that her daughter Thérèse followed in her life, but which she had to reintroduce to a Carmel that had failed to follow this advice.

Mother Geneviève was 81 years old when Thérèse entered. Thérèse described how, as she stepped over the cloister threshold, she was taken to the Choir which was in darkness because there was Exposition of the Blessed Sacrament—it was in darkness so that, with the grilles open, the sisters could not be seen from those in the chapel on the other side. She was led to where Mother Geneviève was sitting; all she could see was two kindly eyes looking down at her as the elderly Carmelite gave the young postulant her blessing. Thérèse knew that she had an advocate in her, because Canon Delatroëtte, when he had adamantly opposed Thérèse's entry, had visited her in the infirmary to ask her opinion about so young a child entering Carmel. Mother Geneviève gave Thérèse her support, ever since she had received Sister Agnès during her last term of office as Prioress, and had a high opinion of the Martin sisters—something that annoyed the Canon exceedingly.

Thérèse herself soon came to appreciate the saintly nun, although Mother Geneviève was already very ill and confined to her bed in the Infirmary. Thérèse was permitted to visit her on occasion, and, during her hard postulancy longed to receive some spiritual help, guidance and consolation from her. She says that at that time she found it hard to open herself to others; at home, she had had Marie to guide her, but now she was determined to follow the Rule and have only that contact with her and Pauline that she would have with any other sister. Thérèse describes herself as having a beleaguered soul as she adapted herself to her new environment and needed help. She was unable to open herself to her Novice Mistress, Mother Marie of the Angels, who, although well-meaning, was at that time unable to understand her. The love she had received from Mother Marie de Gonzague before she entered had now changed to sternness, even harshness.

In this state of mind, Thérèse went one day to visit the sick nun but found two sisters already with her. Thérèse smiled at her and went to leave but Mother Geneviève called her back, saying, 'Wait, my little child, I'm going to say just a little word to you; every time you come you ask for a spiritual bouquet. Well, today, I will give you this one: Serve God with peace and joy; remember that our God is a God of peace'. Thérèse was nearly in tears as she left the room. She had felt herself in such darkness that she had been wondering whether God loved her, and these gentle words came as a balm to her soul. She felt sure that Mother Geneviève must have received some revelation as to her state of soul, but when she visited the nun the following Sunday Mother Geneviève assured her that she had not. 'And then my admiration was greater still when I saw the degree to which Jesus was living within her and making her act and speak. That type of sanctity seems the truest and the most holy to me, and it is the type that I desire because in it one meets with no deception.'[4]

This reflection is important because it describes beautifully Thérèse's own experience when later she came to instruct her novices. She found that somehow she, too, was given just the right words to say to her novices that she was sure didn't come from her.

During her final illness Thérèse tried to conceal the severity of her condition for as long as possible, and in this she had Mother Geneviève as an example. For thirty years she had borne without complaint the internal growth; sometimes her sisters would find her unconscious on the floor, and one time during the winter she had gone out to the garden to see to the enclosure door but had fainted. Sister Adelaide, working in her cell, heard a voice telling her to go into the garden. There she found her Prioress unconscious, who would have died of exposure in the severe cold if she had not been found. During her later years she developed dropsy and senile gangrene that infected all her limbs. Despite that, she retained her sweetness and gentleness to the end, an uncomplaining patient.

If her sufferings were not enough in themselves, Mother Geneviève did not seek for ease. She still sat on the backless wooden stool for as long as she was able, only eventually accepting a hard wooden chair with a back. When she became completely incapacitated, an armchair was made for her but it still had to be hard, according to her instructions. However, the back was so high that she was unable to sit in it properly, but had to sit on the edge sideways; everyone thought that was how she liked it. When, after several years, it had to be mended, a soft, sprung armchair was brought in for her to use. Mother Marie de Gonzague came in to console her for the loss of her armchair for the couple of days it would take to repair it, saying sympathetically, 'How are you going to manage all this time without it, Mother?'

The infirmarian, who was beginning to have doubts as to its comfort, kept her eyes on the invalid and saw her give an involuntary laugh as she saw the humour of the situation, replying that she could manage for a few days. The sister went to the Prioress afterwards and tried to persuade her that the old Mother would really be much more comfortable in the replacement chair. Mother Gonzague, though, was unpersuaded, and the invalid kept her uncomfortable chair to the end.

That sweetness was undimmed when she received the occasional rebuff from Mother Marie de Gonzague. The Prioress appreciated the sick nun's holiness but came into the infirmary one day very annoyed because she had given some advice which had proved a problem. 'I beg of you not to interfere in the business of the house,' she said to her in the presence of a young sister who had been reading to the invalid. 'You don't know what is going on, and your advice is worse than useless.'

'Thank you, dear Mother,' was Mother Geneviève's response, 'it is a great charity to tell me so. When one has been Prioress, one is inclined to interfere in matters that no longer concern one! It is quite true that I cannot see what is going on, and I may make foolish mistakes. Please forgive me!'

Her infirmarian was amazed that her patient had lost none of her habitual calm, and when the Prioress had left the room Mother Geneviève simply asked her, with a gentle smile, to continue her reading.

On 22 July 1881 she celebrated her Golden Jubilee of Profession, and on that same day in 1890 she celebrated 60 years of her Clothing. This milestone was not normally commemorated, only that of Profession, but with her health so precarious it was feared she would not live to see 1891 and her 60 years of Profession. She had received Extreme Unction for the second time on Good Friday of that year and was now completely confined to her bed in the infirmary. For the festivities she wore the same crown of roses that she had worn for these ceremonies fifty years before; both Sister Agnès and Sister Marie had also worn it for their own Professions. For some reason Mother Agnès passed it on to Céline for safe keeping, as a precious relic. However, Mother Geneviève did live to celebrate her Diamond Jubilee of Profession, and Céline sent fish, cherries and cakes to help towards the celebrations.

Despite her infirmity, Thérèse says that she was a great help to the Martin sisters as they went through the suffering of their father's protracted illness and she also helped Thérèse when she made her Profession. Thérèse describes how, on the eve of the ceremony she was plagued by the thought that her vocation was a sham, a dream, a chimera. She was convinced that Carmel was not for her. She approached both her Novice Mistress who assured her that her fears were groundless, and the Prioress, who simply laughed at her. She then discussed those temptations with Mother Geneviève, who revealed that she had had just the same temptations, which was just the consolation Thérèse needed for her peace of mind.

Mother Geneviève died 5 December 1891, and the event made a deep impression on Thérèse. In her letters it became a marker for other events such as her own Profession and the severe epidemic of influenza that hit the community later that month. As the death agony began, the community was summoned to her bedside, and Thérèse was placed at the foot of the bed to witness everything. It was the first time she had witnessed someone dying, because at the death of her own mother she was kept away and saw her only in her coffin. It seemed not to have occurred to Agnès or Marie that it might have been too traumatic for a sensitive young seventeen year old, who had experienced such suffering at the loss of her own mother, but in the event it was perhaps another form of 'closure' for Thérèse. During the two hours she spent before Mother Geneviève's bed, instead of being filled with fervour she felt just a numbness, but as the elderly nun drew her last breath Thérèse suddenly experienced an inexpressible joy and fervour; it was as if Mother Geneviève was sharing with the young sister an inkling of the bliss she now experienced in heaven, being with the Lord she had loved and served so faithfully on earth. Thérèse herself was convinced that she went straight to heaven. Earlier, convinced of the nun's sanctity, Thérèse had said to her that perhaps she would not go to purgatory, and Mother Geneviève said with her customary gentleness and sweetness, 'I hope not'.

Such sweetness was often not passed on to the sisters. When the coffin was taken down to the Choir Thérèse helped to lay out flowers on the bier. 'Oh yes,' observed a lay sister, 'you manage very well to move the big wreathes from your relatives to the front and keep the modest ones from poor people in the back!' Thérèse said nothing, but with a sweet smile moved an inexpensive wreath of moss to the front.

Standing before the bier was cathartic for Thérèse, because it seemed so much smaller than the bier in which her mother had been laid, and which had seemed so big and threatening to a small child. But the bed in which Mother Geneviève died was also the bed in which Thérèse herself would die, and this reflection later played on her mind as she battled with her sickness and spiritual darkness.

However, there was a consolation for her; earlier, before the bier was brought down to the Choir, the sisters were eager to take some small item as a relic of one whom they revered as a saint. Thérèse had observed a small tear rest on the dead nun's cheek, a token of the agony of her last moments. Thérèse later crept into the Choir and wiped the tear away with a piece of cloth, which she treasured as a relic, placing it in the small New Testament that she kept always with her. She also kept a small daisy from the posy of flowers that was placed in the dead nun's hands, and sent it to Céline as a token of Mother Geneviève's blessing.

Mother Geneviève had appreciated the sterling qualities she had observed in Sister Agnès and prophesied that she would one day be Prioress. This came true two years later when Agnès was elected Prioress. Canon Delatroëtte recalled her example in the exhortation he gave the community after the election:

> Your saintly Mother Geneviève will aid you, you will apply yourself to imitating the precious example she left you. I can tell you without failing in discretion that if the greater part of your Sisters thought of giving you their votes, it is because they noticed you are trying to practice the virtues you saw practiced in her.[5]

Mother Geneviève appreciated Mother Agnès and was well looked after by Marie, but she had a special place in her heart for the youngest sister. One night shortly after her death Thérèse dreamt that Mother Geneviève 'was making her last will and testament, giving each of the Sisters something which she possessed. When my turn finally came, I thought I would get nothing as there was really nothing left to give; however, she said: 'To you I leave my *heart,*' repeated three times with great emphasis.[6]

This is surely the most precious lasting legacy Mother Geneviève could leave, and one that was received a hundredfold by Thérèse, her most famous daughter.

Notes

1 Lisieux Carmel, *The Foundation of the Carmel of Lisieux and its Foundress Reverend Mother Geneviève of St Teresa 1913* (USA: Kessinger Publishing, 2007), (facsimile), translated by a Religious of the Society of the Holy Child Jesus, p. 38.

2 *Ibid.,* p. 43.

3 Quoted in H. Clarke OCarm, *Messenger of Love* (Faversham, UK: Carmelite Press, 1976), p. 46.

4 Thérèse of Lisieux, *Story of a Soul* (Washington DC: ICS Publications, 1976), translated by J. Clarke OCD, pp. 169–170.

5 Thérèse of Lisieux, *Letters Vol 11.* (Washington DC: ICS Publications, 1988), translated by J. Clarke OCD, p. 782, note 6.

6 Thérèse of Lisieux, *Story of a Soul,* p. 171.

6

MOTHER MARIE DE GONZAGUE

PRIORESS

IN BIOGRAPHIES OF Saint Thérèse Mother Marie de Gonzague, who was Prioress for most of her time in Carmel, has often been portrayed as the wicked witch who caused Thérèse much suffering. It is true that she treated Thérèse very harshly during her novitiate, but with such a complex character as that of Mother Marie de Gonzague, there is much more to be said.

Marie de Gonzague, in the world Marie-Adèle Rosalie Davy de Virville, was born at Caen in 1834, of an aristocratic family. She entered the Lisieux Carmel 29 November 1860, received the habit 30 May 1861 and was Professed 27 June 1862.

She was elected Subprioress in 1866 and for a second term in 1869; three years later she was elected to her first term as Prioress. Such a rapid rise in the little Carmel is a testimony to the outstanding gifts she had, as well as her character that was destined to govern, even with all its faults and shortcomings.

She first met Thérèse in the parlour when Pauline was seeking entrance into the community and was immediately taken by the angelic looking little girl, nicknaming her Theresita, the name of Saint Teresa of Avila's young niece. The letters she wrote to Thérèse at this time were full of affection and loving admonitions to look after her health, which was suffering due to Pauline's entry into Carmel. She was well aware of Thérèse's desire to enter Carmel, but once this became a distinct possibility when Thérèse was only fifteen, she wavered in her support, sometimes favouring it, at other times, with good reason, against it. She was well aware that it was unusual and against the Constitutions to have too many members of the same family in one community, and that with Marie and Pauline members of the Chapter, Thérèse would not be able to be a voting member of the Chapter. She was also well aware of the precarious nature of Thérèse's health—she suffered from frequent headaches, and, in the winter, from colds and chest complaints—and of course her age. She knew that their Chaplain, Canon Delatroëtte, was adamantly opposed to the idea, as well as that of the bishop, Mgr Hugonin.

Canon Delatroëtte was well aware of the spiritual health, or lack of it, of the Lisieux community, as well as the volatile nature of Mother Marie de Gonzague herself, and would well have wondered how a young girl would fare under her direction. He had once remarked that if the outside world knew her they would burn the convent down! Despite all this, by the time Thérèse came to make the famous pilgrimage to Rome and the plan was hatched for Thérèse to make her petition to the Pope himself, it was Mother Marie de Gonzague who framed what she would say.

After her entry into Carmel Thérèse found a Prioress who was very different from the kindly person she had met in the parlour. With her violent mood swings Mother Marie de Gonzague could erupt in outbursts that rocked the convent, but she could also be charming and charismatic. Many priests who visited the

Carmel had a great regard for her and sought her spiritual advice. The photographs of her do not do justice to her attractiveness and commanding presence. Many of the sisters had an uncritical adulation for her, and she cultivated this entourage like the *grande dame* she was. She had favourites whom she could drop without warning. Thérèse herself was not immune from this charm and describes how, as a novice, she had to hold on to the banisters when passing her room in order not to give in to herself and knock on the door for a crumb of comfort from the Prioress.

She also describes, with some humour against herself, of an incident when she was Portress and had to hand back the keys of the enclosure to Mother Marie de Gonzague, who was ill at the time. The sister looking after the Prioress did not want Thérèse to go in and hand over the keys in person; Thérèse wanted to do so in order to have just that small contact with her. Her inner struggle was so violent that, when she overcame herself and handed the keys to the sister, she had to go and sit on the stairs for a while to gain her composure.

As a postulant Thérèse was not expected to follow the daily horarium completely and was given exemptions. In November, she was given permission to ask her relatives for some fur-lined slippers, and the weekly visits of the family continued. One of the contradictions in Mother Marie de Gonzague's character was that she was strict in some respects but lax in others. She was drawn to extreme penances (ordering that a clump of nettles should not cut down so that she could use them for this purpose), and yet the rules for visits, letter writing, keeping the monastic silence, for example, could be broken at will. It was to her credit, though, that she saw the need the Martin family had to give each other support in the trials they were going through, and permitted the rules to be relaxed.

If she broke the rules on family visits for the Martin family, she was even more lax when it concerned her own family and with less reason. Gossip about her aristocratic relatives was standard fare at recreations. Her sister, a Countess, unhappily married, would arrive at all hours, and the whole community was commandeered to provide every comfort that she required, however much disruption it caused to community life. Thérèse herself was not immune to the demands made on the sisters on her behalf and recounted that one evening, she was told to prepare a lamp for the Countess during the great silence. She had such a violent reaction that she questioned the authority of the Prioress to demand this of her, and yet this response ran against all her instincts of obedience. She had to overcome her sense of grievance by imagining that she was preparing it for the Holy Family, and was in this way able to keep her emotions in check. It can only be imagined the effect such abuse of authority had on sisters less holy than Thérèse.

Mother Marie de Gonzague would give orders that were often irrational, and then forget them the next day, or she would contradict herself with a different order later on. The sisters would judiciously ignore them and carry on as usual, which did not contribute to the respect they had for the Prioress, or for the good running of the community.

Only Thérèse kept these orders, even at great inconvenience. For example, the Prioress one day forbade the sisters from using the Choir as a short cut to some of the offices; the rest of the community gradually went back to their old ways, and only

Thérèse continued to obey the injunction, however inconvenient it was. She was well aware of the Prioress' faults, but was determined that she should keep her standards as a religious. To her, Mother Marie de Gonzague was her 'good Mother' and expressed the will of God for her.

The Prioress did indeed treat her harshly as a postulant and novice, correcting her every perceived fault, but this was perhaps to balance what she saw as the dangers for Thérèse in the cloister. As the youngest in the community, and a very young girl, she could easily have become the pet of the community, especially as her two sisters tried to shield her from the hardships of the life as much as they could. While the community benefited from the almost daily gifts of fish, cakes and sweets M Martin showered on them, they were also jealous of Thérèse for being the occasion of the largesse, especially as he had bought them on behalf of his 'little queen'.

However, Mother Marie de Gonzague was a shrewd judge of character and she soon discerned that Thérèse was dealing with all these difficulties in a way that was exceptional. As we have seen, the Prioress tacitly gave her permission to have contact with her two sisters in a way that would normally not occur, as novices were not fully integrated into the community. Thérèse quietly but firmly adhered the rules of silence and did not allow herself to indulge in the conversations that she would dearly love to have had with them.

When Pauline tried to remonstrate with the Prioress about her treatment of Thérèse, Mother Marie de Gonzague responded that she knew what she was doing, and she did. She perhaps knew the stuff of which Thérèse was made better than anyone, better even than Pauline, and later Thérèse acknowledged that the treatment that she was given at the beginning of her religious life had strengthened and matured her.

Given her character, it is understandable that Marie de Gonzague tried to cling on to power after Agnès of Jesus' election as Prioress, since she had been in that position for so long, but despite her timidity Agnès had the integrity of all the Martin sisters. She had high expectations of the religious life, and she wanted to govern in her own way and try to rectify some of the abuses within the community.

When Mother Agnès was almost obliged to nominate Marie de Gonzague as Novice Mistress, but knowing her moody and volatile nature made the surprise decision to appoint Thérèse as her assistant, Thérèse asked her, and Agnés agreed that, instead of leaving the Novitiate after her three years of Profession, she should remain as 'head novice', which gave her the opportunity to guide the novices. The young sisters were well aware of the situation, and it delighted them that they could go to Thérèse rather than the ex-Prioress, whom they nicknamed *'le loup'*, the wolf, however much Thérèse tried to instil respect for her in them.

For all her faults, it is to Marie de Gonzague's credit that she did not object to this arrangement, although Thérèse had to walk a very narrow tightrope of tact and judiciousness. The ex-prioress would sometimes contradict what Thérèse had told the novices and countermand her instructions. Nevertheless, she fully understood the steely character of the young sister, describing her in a letter to the Prioress of the Tours Carmel, on the occasion of her Profession, as 'a child I offered to God yesterday. This angelic seventeen-year-old has the judgment of a thirty-year-old, the religious perfection of an old and accomplished novice, and self-mastery. She is a perfect nun.'[1]

New elections were due to be held at the beginning of 1896. The old Prioress was determined to be re-elected and lobbied vigorously for this outcome, and she was also determined, as we have seen, that Sister Mary of the Blessed Trinity and Sister Geneviève should make their profession under her, and tried to have the ceremonies postponed. To postpone a Profession for this reason was profoundly wrong and irregular, but it was not the only occasion when Mother Marie de Gonzague would defy the rules, even when she had no right to do so. Thérèse recounts how helped she was during a retreat given by the Franciscan, Fr Alexis, and would have loved to speak to him again. But the Prioress, perhaps through the jealousy that was one of her characteristics, refused permission, and Thérèse, who was sacristan at the time, had to see all the other sisters go into the confessional, apart from her. Not that the others sisters were allowed unlimited access. During retreat times, Mother Marie de Gonzague would mount a veritable surveillance on the retreat giver's confessional; according to the sisters' testimony, she couldn't bear to see them staying there too long.[2]

Again, it was a time when the Pope was encouraging his flock to go to more frequent communion, even at every Mass, but Mother Marie de Gonzague would not allow this, out of reverence, as she saw it, for the Sacrament. Thérèse was deeply hurt by this, and said to the Prioress that after her death this permission would be given. Only a few days after her death and with the advent of a new chaplain, the community were at last allowed to receive daily communion.

The ballot for Prioress at the elections went to seven ballots before Mother Marie de Gonzague was elected by only one vote. She did not appoint Mother Agnès as Novice Mistress, keeping this role for herself, and even forced her to stay outside the Chapter door while the voting took place. The weeks and months following the elections left the community in disarray. In June, Thérèse wrote a remarkable letter[3] to her Prioress that hints at some of the problems, but also the extraordinary relationship that she, a twenty year old novice, had with the older nun. Mother Agnès testified that Mother Marie de Gonzague was not upset by the letter and that, 'Basically, it was in Thérèse alone that she had any confidence; the other nuns seemed to be traitors to her'.[4]

In the letter Thérèse described her Prioress as a shepherdess and herself as a little lamb, and that the shepherdess confided in the little lamb 'as though the lamb were her equal'. The shepherdess 'confided to it her troubles and at times shed tears with it.' Mother Marie de Gonzague had wanted to be re-elected, but now, feeling she had lost the confidence of nearly half the community, when before, according to Thérèse, the voting had been unanimous, it was a bitter chalice. Speaking as to Jesus, Thérèse has the little lamb say to him, 'Could You not, then, give the staff to another, just as my dear Mother desired, or if you wanted absolutely to place it again in her hands, why did You not do so after the first deliberation?' This hint that the Prioress was now regretting being elected is echoed in a letter she wrote in April to the Prioress of the Compiègne Carmel:

> A little prayer for the poor old woman upon whose shoulders they have placed the staff

> again in the month of March. She would so much have preferred to remain in her dear solitude because the burden seems heavier to her than in the past. The three years in the cell appeared to me like three days![5]

At this time the Prioress was sixty two years old and in ill health. Although robust, she suffered from frequent bouts of pneumonia, but the burden would have been lighter if she knew she had the backing of most of the community.

Thérèse hints that on one side were nuns who were judging the situation from a purely human, worldly, standpoint of satisfaction and on the other side those whom Thérèse calls the 'dear sheep', her own sisters, who were making their disappointment clear at not seeing Mother Agnès re-elected. Even Thérèse, on entering the Choir after the election and seeing Mother Marie de Gonzague installed in the Prioress' stall, could not help a look of surprise passing over her face, so convinced had she been that her sister would be re-elected.

Thérèse answers her own question as to why the Lord had allowed such a fraught election to take place by saying, very delicately, that it was a trial from which her Prioress could profit. She would not do anything to take this time of trial away from her and quotes from a sentence inscribed on the wall at the foot of the stairs leading to the cells of the sisters: 'To lift oneself up, one must place his foot on the steps of creatures and attach himself to Me only.' While not being blind to her Prioress' faults, she was very delicately hinting that Marie de Gonzague could use these trials to detach herself from her unhealthy reliance on the very human affection of some of the sisters and grow in her reliance on God alone. Thérèse also implies that the older nun was upset by what she saw as mitigations of the rule and had said that 'primitive spirit of our flock is going away' under Mother Agnès' term of office. She agrees that a worldly spirit is abroad, but pointed out that true mortification is the interior one, not the exterior mortifications to which she was so attached.

Not that the Prioress was oblivious of her failings. During one retreat, Sister Teresa of St Augustine came out from the parlour after a talk with the retreat giver, in great distress because he had told her that she had one foot in hell. 'Don't worry about that,' was Mother Marie de Gonzague's reply, 'I already have two feet in hell!'

When Mother Agnès was eventually told of the seriousness of Thérèse's illness and was faced with the thought of her immanent death, she wanted Thérèse to write about her years in Carmel. The problem was that she had not told the Prioress of the existence of the first notebook, and knowing Marie de Gonzague's volatility, was fearful of her reaction. Finally, plucking up her courage, she knocked on the Prioress' door after Matins, at nearly midnight on 2 June. Mother Agnès gave her account of what she said:

> Mother, it is impossible for me to sleep before confiding a secret to you. When I was Prioress Sister Thérèse wrote for me, to please me and under obedience, some memories of her childhood. I re-read them the other day. They are good, but you would not be able to draw a great deal from them to help you with her circular after her death, for there is almost nothing about her religious life. If you commanded her to do it, she could write something more serious, and no doubt you would have something incomparably better than I have.[6]

That last sentence was a shrewd one, pandering to the Prioress' vanity, and it had the desired effect. The following day, Mother Marie de Gonzague gave Thérèse a notebook with the necessary command to keep writing.

During her term of office, Mother Agnès had also given Thérèse a young seminarian who would later enter the White Fathers, Maurice Bellière, as a 'spiritual brother', whom she would support with her prayers and sacrifices as he studied for the priesthood. At the end of May, after the elections, Mother Marie de Gonzague received a letter from Fr Adolphe Roulland of the Foreign Missions, who wanted a sister to write to him and support him in his mission. The Prioress assured him of the support of her prayers, for she had a strong missionary spirit herself, but passed over the responsibility to Thérèse to write to him. She was well aware of that same burning missionary zeal in her beloved daughter.

When Thérèse was eventually installed in the infirmary Mother Marie de Gonzague tried to give her the best of attention and what medicine she could, apart from morphine which would have eased her pain. Her sisters, however, were secretly able to give her liquid morphine towards the end. The old Prioress was devastated by Thérèse's increasing sickness. 'This poor Mother began to weep hot tears when she began the *Salve Regina* this Saturday,' Mother Agnès wrote to the Guérins on 7 June, a day when Thérèse was very sick. Even so, there were difficult moments. On several occasions Thérèse was made to feel her Prioress's jealousy which flared up because the novices often went to the infirmary to see her. Just a few days before she died, Mother Marie de Gonzague spoke to her so coldly and made her visits so brief that Thérèse asked one of the novices: 'do you know what I have done to upset Our Mother?'

'I know', replied the novice, 'but I did not wish to tell you lest I caused you pain. Our Mother has noticed that I love you very much and that I am very happy when I can come and see you and she said to me: "If I had known of your close ties with Sister Thérèse of the Child Jesus and how she suffices for you in everything, I would not have worried about you".' Thérèse replied simply, 'Ah! That's the reason. Thank you.'

The community doctor, Dr De Cornière stubbornly refused to agree that Thérèse had tuberculosis, but Mother Marie de Gonzague was afraid to upset him by bringing in another doctor. However, when he went on holiday she asked Dr Néele, the Guérins brother-in-law, to come and examine her. He was horrified to see the state Thérèse was in and rounded on Mother Marie de Gonzague for what he thought was her neglect. She in turn lost her temper, railing against the whole family, as well as Thérèse herself, in Thérèse's presence.

Thérèse died 30 September, and Mother Marie de Gonzague wrote later of her profound grief at losing 'her treasure'. She wrote to Fr Madeleine a month later: 'The last events that have taken place here have left me almost lifeless. I don't know where I am or where I'm going. The death of our angel has left a void in me that will never be filled.'[7]

Now there was the death notice to be dealt with. It had already been agreed that this would be the book, but knowing Mother Marie de Gonzague's sensitivity, Mother Agnès changed the dedication of Thérèse's account of her childhood, and also the letter written to

Sister Marie of the Sacred Heart, so that it seemed as if the whole of the book had been addressed to the Prioress.

Mother Marie de Gonzague's health was failing, and when elections came up in April 1902, her six years as Prioress came to an end and Mother Agnès was again elected. The following year, Mother Marie de Gonzague was diagnosed with cancer of the tongue and her health deteriorated rapidly. She was moved into the infirmary, into the same bed in which Thérèse had died.

Their differences were now all forgotten, and Mother Agnès nursed her old adversary devotedly, often staying by her bedside and gave her all the alleviation she could, although Mother Marie de Gonzague steadfastly refused morphine for herself, just as it had not been given to Thérèse. On 17 December, she had looked at Mother Agnès and said, 'I have offended God more than anyone else in the community. I should not hope to be saved if I did not have my little Thérèse to intercede for me.' These were to be the last words she was able to utter.

Even as a novice, Mother Marie de Gonzague stated that Thérèse would make an excellent Prioress. She saw in Thérèse, too, the Prioress that she herself, with all her faults and undisciplined temperament, could never be. Marie de Gonzague said that Thérèse's only fault was her three sisters, but, unlike the Prioress, Thérèse purified and sanctified her relationships with her sisters, at very great cost to herself; her love would extend to all her sisters in religion, in a way that Mother Marie de Gonzague was unable to do with her own family ties and with her favourites in the community. She needed the adulation of others and allowed unhealthy attachments to form, whereas Thérèse carried out her duties as novice mistress without fear or favour, with the love of Christ Himself. Thérèse showed her that external mortification was worthless without interior mortification.

Thérèse, was, as it were, a mirror held up to her, showing what she should have been, but it is to the credit of the Prioress that far from resenting it, she found in Thérèse the only one in whom she could confide, in whom she had complete trust. For her part, Thérèse revered her, not only as the one to whom God had given her as her authority for his will for her on earth, but with a genuine affection and love. She was surely there with her prayers at the end to ensure that her old Prioress did not, after all, have 'two feet in hell'.

Notes

1 G. Gaucher, *The Spiritual Journey of St Thérese of Lisieux* (London: Darton Longman and Todd, 1989), p. 112.

2 J. Vinatier, *Mère Agnès de Jesus* (Paris: Les Editions du Cerf, 1993), p. 134.

3 Thérèse of Lisieux, *Letters Vol 11.* (Washington DC: ICS Publications, 1988), translated by J. Clarke OCD, p. 958.

4 *Ibid.*

5 *Ibid.*, p. 962.

6 Gaucher, *The Spiritual Journey,* p. 186.

7 J.-F. Six, *Light of the Night* (London: SCM Press Ltd, 1996), p. 197.

7

MOTHER MARIE OF THE ANGELS

NOVICE MISTRESS

WHEN THÉRÈSE ENTERED Carmel her Novice Mistress was Mother Marie of the Angels, at the time forty three years of age.

Born Jeanne de Chaumontel in 1845 in Montpinçon, Calvados, she was the only sister of aristocratic background in the community, apart from Mother Marie de Gonzague. She entered Carmel 29 October 1866, received the habit 19 March 1867 and after a difficult Novitiate, was professed 25 March 1867. Ida Gorrës described her[1] as lacking in prudence and objectivity, with overflowing emotions, lacking discrimination and insight into souls, fluttery and distracted and wearisomely loquacious towards her novices—the loquaciousness that Sister Agnès found difficult to cope with during her own novitiate.

If it was true that she had these negative characteristics, she certainly had an insight into Thérèse's soul; Thérèse described her as a saint of the old school, and she had sterling qualities as well. Aristocratic and fearless, she also had virtues that Thérèse would have appreciated: a genuine love of poverty, of silence—despite her loquaciousness when the Rule permitted speaking!—real humility and a deep spirit of prayer. It was these qualities for which she was first elected

Subprioress from 1883 for two six year terms until 1899, as well as her kindness and tactfulness, always concerned in making peace. Being Subprioress under the rule of Mother Marie de Gonzague would surely have tried and honed these attributes to the full.

Mother Marie of the Angels was also appointed Novice Mistress in 1886, a position she filled until 1893 when Thérèse was given the post; she took it up again after Thérèse's death, until 1909. So when Thérèse entered she had had several years of guiding young people in the Carmelite way of life.

She first met Thérèse in the parlour after Pauline entered and was struck by the nine year old child. 'I could easily see that this beautiful child was blessed by God,' she testified at the hearing into Thérèse's sanctity. 'Whenever I was near her the effect it had on me was similar to what one feels before the tabernacle. She radiated an atmosphere of calm, silence, gentleness and purity that made me regard her with a very real respect'[2]

Mother Marie of the Angels had an equally high regard for her after Thérèse had entered, because she had never had a postulant who was so perfect in every way. Even at that age, she said, Thérèse could easily become prioress, let alone novice mistress. She admired the way Thérèse met the challenges and difficulties of her new life with courage and determination, though unaware that she herself was the cause of much of the young postulant's sufferings. As Thérèse described in her autobiography, the novice mistress was very absent-minded, giving her charges instructions and then forgetting what she had told them. One of these was that Thérèse should tell her whenever she felt ill, and since she suffered daily from stomach pains, perhaps due to the strain of adapting to her new life, Thérèse reported these every day, even though she would much rather have borne them without complaint. This led to Mother Marie of the Angels speaking of them to the Prioress, with both of them doubting whether Thérèse was strong enough for the life.

Another time she accused Thérèse falsely of breaking a vase, an accusation that Thérèse bore without excusing herself. When Mother Mary of the Angels read in Thérèse's autobiography that she had almost died of the cold in bed in the winter, she deeply regretted that Thérèse had never asked for extra blankets, because she would have been given them. It was perhaps a sign of the Novice Mistress's absent-mindedness that she herself never thought to ask Thérèse if she needed them.

At the beginning Thérèse had difficulty in explaining her state of soul, but described without complaint her dryness in prayer and the suffering Mother Marie de Gonzague's harshness caused her. At one point this was so overwhelming that Thérèse flung herself into her Novice Mistress's arms for comfort.

There was one sister who understood her difficulty in opening herself up—Sister Fébronie, at that time Subprioress. One day during recreation, she turned laughingly to Thérèse, saying, 'My child, it seems you don't have very much to tell your Superiors.'

'Why do you say that, Mother?'

'Because your soul is extremely simple, but when you will be perfect, you will be even more simple; the closer one approaches to God, the simpler one becomes.'

Thérèse recognised the truth of this and it eased her peace of mind about her difficulties. When, in November 1889, Thérèse was told that her Profession would be delayed because of her youth, Mother Marie of the

Angels fully appreciated Thérèse's attitude of acceptance of God's will for her, after her initial bitter disappointment. She was on retreat at the time and Thérèse was receiving instruction from Mother Marie de Gonzague, but the Novice Mistress kept in touch with her by writing a beautiful letter[3] to her novice, her 'Benjamin', encouraging Thérèse in her acceptance of the cross: 'May divine suffering be the centre of your life; plunge into this bottomless ocean, and may it engulf you as it did Jesus, for there alone are life and happiness'. She obviously recognised the spiritual maturity of her young novice, to feed her such strong meat. She ended the note with a paragraph that reveals how much she loved and admired Thérèse:

> Take flight to the All of your heart with wings of humility, simplicity and love. Jesus loves you with a tender predilection, so pay Him in return, and be happy to love Jesus in suffering for Jesus! I am not forgetting my dear little Benjamin, and, soon, we shall see one another; in the meanwhile, profit well from all the good talks our beloved Mother will give you. Much more than I, she is Jesus for you, and, better than I, will know how to speak about Him and make Him loved by you.

In Thérèse's desolation at this time, Mother Marie of the Angels could assure her, that, 'Yes, my beloved little daughter, Jesus is very, very much pleased with you.'[4]

In the letter she calls Thérèse a little grain of sand, a thought that Thérèse loved for its littleness and hiddenness and used herself in letters to Céline, especially. In another letter Mother Marie of the Angels wrote to her a few days later she calls her a reed, an emblem that was put on her clothing—a different emblem was assigned to each sister so that their clothing could be distinguished as to whose it was. It was also an emblem that meant a lot to Mother Marie of the Angels, something she gleaned from the writings of Sister Marie of St Pièrre, of the Tours Carmel, who promulgated devotion to the Holy Face, and whose writings the Novice Mistress loved to read.

In it, she assures Thérèse of how much she is loved by Jesus, and of her own love for her young novice, and at the same time discerns that Thérèse is destined to follow Jesus in the way of the Cross:

> Little reed, infinitely loved by Jesus and profoundly dear to my heart!... Jesus does not will any joys for you!... Why are you surprised by this?... Isn't this what He chose for Himself and the lot He gave to His Immaculate Mother? Isn't it the lot of His love ones, His predestined?

She goes on to say, 'We are nothing, but Jesus is all, we have nothing, but He has all! We can do nothing, but He can do all and for all if we are really convinced that we can do nothing!'

We can perhaps see in what her Novice Mistress tells her here, the seeds of Thérèse's 'Little Way'; she would have taken these words deeply into her soul. It was the basis of her whole spirituality that she came to God with empty hands, because everything she was, all that she did, all that she had, came from God. However, the genius of Thérèse was that she would almost turn this thought upside down and take this conviction further, with a boldness that frightened Mother Agnès. Yes, Thérèse was as insignificant as a grain of sand, but at the same time she had the incomparable dignity of being a child of God her Father. Therefore, since she was his child who had nothing of herself, but had God as her Father who possessed all things, so Thérèse could approach her heavenly Father with empty hands but with a confident, joyful boldness that he would give her everything she needed. Even more, she had seen for herself that God would indulge even her slightest wish, such as sending her snow on her Clothing day or give her back in Carmel's enclosure the wild flowers she had so loved in her walks in the countryside.

The following year, Mother Marie of the Angels was able to rejoice with Thérèse as she made her Profession 8 September, Feast of the Birthday of Our Lady. She composed the verses sung at Recreation to celebrate her beloved novice's betrothal, and in a note adds, 'Your poor little mistress who wants you to be a saint, a great saint, and who loves you so tenderly.'[5]

Earlier that year, Thérèse had confided to Fr Blino, a Jesuit who was preaching the community retreat, that she wanted to become a saint, saying; 'I want to love God as much as Saint Teresa.' To Fr Blino this was pride and presumption, but Thérèse was more of a theologian than the priest, quoting in response Jesus himself when he said, 'be perfect as your Father in heaven is perfect'. Here in this letter, Marie of the Angels understood her novice's desires, and that they were something to which she could rightfully aspire, recognising the same desires in herself. She perhaps recognised, too, a greater holiness in Thérèse than she possessed, and was humble in the recognition.

Once Mother Marie de Gonzague became Novice Mistress after Pauline's election as Prioress, Mother Mary of the Angels was relieved of her post in favour of her erstwhile novice, and her relationship with Thérèse became that of any other sister in the community. Nevertheless, by this time there was a greater understanding between the two of them and Thérèse was given permission to discuss her spiritual progress with her and, surely, since Thérèse had been given the task of Novice Mistress, her advice, too. What Marie of the Angels discerned, and what she valued in Thérèse, can give an indication of her own spiritual life. She could appreciate the depths of Thérèse's love of poverty, of silence and humility, because these were her own characteristics.

When she was seventeen and eighteen Thérèse studied the works Saint John of the Cross, which were at that time her main source of spiritual nourishment. As she discussed her thoughts on his writings with her Novice Mistress, who knew his works well, the older nun was amazed at her novice's understanding of the great Carmelite's teaching.

When she was no longer Novice Mistress, Mother Marie of the Angels was appointed sacristan, which meant she had to deal with the very awkward sister, Teresa of St Augustine. Thérèse had also deliberately asked to work with this sister, precisely because her difficult character and explosive temper had alienated all the other sisters. Thérèse won her over so completely that when she proved too much for her to cope with, Mother Marie of the Angels turned to Thérèse who was able to calm her down.

After Thérèse's death Mother Marie of the Angels flung herself wholeheartedly into supporting her cause for canonisation, knowing from first hand how completely her former charge was eligible for it. She spread Thérèse's message to her friends and relations, and was herself the recipient of many graces from Thérèse. She reported that quite frequently, sweet-smelling perfumes permeated the cloisters. She resumed the task of Novice Mistress after Thérèse's death until 1909, and could therefore form a new influx of novices in her former charge's teaching. She died 24 November 1924.

Notes

1 I. F. Gorrës, *The Hidden Face* (London: Burns & Oates, 1959), p. 196.

2 C. O'Mahoney OCD (ed.), *St Therese of Lisieux by Those Who Knew Her* (Dublin: Veritas Publications, 1975), p. 202.

3 Thérèse of Lisieux, *Letters Vol 1.* (Washington DC: ICS Publications, 1982), translated by J. Clarke OCD p. 595.

4 *Ibid.*, pp. 597–598.

5 *Ibid.*, p. 678.

8

TWO DIFFICULT NOVICES

WHEN THÉRÈSE WAS given charge of the Novitiate, she knew at once that she could not do anything by her own strength. Indeed, the varied and difficult characters of the novices under her charge would have taxed the wisdom of even the most experienced novice mistress. Given that she was only nineteen when she began to be given this oversight is a testimony to her amazing maturity and God-given wisdom. Thérèse describes her approach to her new role in her autobiography.[1]

First of all, she recognised the infinite value in the eyes of God of the souls of her novices: she was 'entering into the sanctuary of souls'. She understood that each soul was different and unique, with differing needs and abilities; there was no such thing as a one size fits all. She knew the task was beyond her, so she had continually to be in a state of receiving, with open hands, and without ever averting her eyes from God, whatever he willed to give to her charges: 'if You wish to give through me what is suitable for each, fill my little hand and without leaving Your arms or turning my head, I shall give Your treasures to the soul who will come and ask for nourishment.'

So successful was God in fulfilling this confidence that the novices were sometimes unnerved by her ability to say exactly the right thing, sometimes even before they had approached her; it gave them the impression that she could see into their souls, something, of course, that Thérèse denied.

She hated the obligation she had to point out their faults to them, but one that she did not shirk. She had to be indifferent to whether they liked her or resented the way she pursued them like a little sheepdog with the sheep in her charge, as she described it. Her peace of soul was undisturbed whatever came her way, and that could be a very difficult thing to achieve for anyone; Thérèse would not compromise or sweeten the pill: 'if she complains and finds bitter what I present, my peace will not be disturbed, and I shall try to convince her this nourishment comes from You and be very careful not to seek any other for her.' It takes a very strong and balanced character not to question whether what she was doing or saying was the right thing or not. Thérèse's confidence came not from her own self-perception but from her deeply grounded humility and her union with God.

That humility allowed her to give the novices free rein in their turn to criticise their novice mistress, and they took full advantage of it. This could have resulted in their having less respect for her, as if it was a weakness in her, but the opposite was true; they had an immense respect for her, discerning that her holiness was of a totally different order to the goodness of some other sisters in the community.

Thérèse imposed hardships on herself that she did not expect from others, and the novices recognised this. Towards the end of her life, remembering how, during the winter, she nearly died from the cold but had said nothing to her superiors, she advised Mother Agnès to make sure that the sisters did not have to go through the same experience.

Sister Marie of the Trinity also gave an example of this. She asked Thérèse whether she could shift from one side to the other when sitting back on her heels during prayer time and recreation. Thérèse looked a little embarrassed and explained that, for herself, after her Clothing, when she was given instruction as to how to sit on her heels, she was told to sit on her left heel. She had faithfully done that ever since, but did not expect that of Marie, who was free to shift her weight as she needed. It was an extra mortification Thérèse took on herself, an expression of her obedience that she did not expect of others. Indeed, the one who had given her the instruction obviously did not expect Thérèse to adhere to it so exactly.

On another occasion, Marie saw that Thérèse was suffering very much from her final illness but was not yet confined to the infirmary, and she tried to persuade her to go to the Prioress and get some dispensations. Thérèse refused, saying that Mother Marie de Gonzague knew of her sickness and would know when to give her the necessary help. The advice Thérèse gave Marie, though, was to go simply to the Prioress, tell her her needs and leave the rest to God.

Thérèse gained the respect and love of her novices, because, however strict she was with them, they knew of the immense love she had for them. She would spare herself nothing to mould them into true Carmelites, however unpromising the material. In one case, though, it seemed that with one of her charges, Sister Marie-Madeleine of the Blessed Sacrament, even a saint was unable to succeed.

Sister Marie-Madeleine of the Blessed Sacrament

Born Mèlanie Le Bon from Plouguenast in the Côte-du-Nord, she entered Carmel 22 July 1892, feast of Saint Mary Magdalene, and took the saint's name. She received the habit 7 September 1893, and since it seems she had no relatives or family, M Guérin was given to her as a godfather, and Mme Alexandre de Virville, Mother Marie de Gonzague's sister-in-law, agreed to be her godmother.

Despite her being accepted for her clothing, the community found her difficult, and Mother Agnès decided that she be put under Thérèse's care to give her extra instruction. She was supposed to meet with Thérèse for half an hour every Sunday, but always went into hiding, so that Thérèse had to spend a frustrating time looking for her. 'Night brings on dark counsels,' Mother Agnès recalled, 'and the following morning, alas! the resolution was taken, unshakeably, not to go seeking Sister Thérèse of the Child Jesus.' The excuse Madeleine gave was that 'When our Mother gives her to us openly as mistress, then I will go, but not before.'[2] This remark is an insight into Thérèse's difficult situation of having only an unofficial role in the Noviciate at the time.

Madeleine had a native intuition, though, and with her quick mind, at the elections of 1893, she saw that Mother Agnès appointed the outgoing Prioress Mother Marie de Gongzague as Novice Mistress only 'to keep the peace', but also that she was 'not able to train novices properly'. When Marie of the Trinity and Madeleine mischievously nicknamed the old Prioress 'the Wolf', Thérèse, she said, 'ceaselessly reminded us that we should see God in our Mother Prioress'—and Madeleine added 'even when the Prioress in question was Mother Marie de Gonzague'![3] The sharp eyes of the novices saw only too clearly her faults.

Before she entered Carmel Madeleine had been a shepherdess, so at her Profession, 20 November 1894, Thérèse composed a long poem for her, entitled, 'The Story of the Shepherdess who Became a Queen' on that theme. She, who had been a poor shepherdess, was now a queen, Thérèse said, because she was now betrothed to Jesus, her King. Thérèse could not help also putting in some advice to her recalcitrant novice—yes, she had some hard times, but she needed to make them her joy; her role was to serve her God, to hide herself, to be the last, advice that Thérèse herself was following to the full in her own life.

Guy Gaucher described Madeleine as 'intelligent, capable and active'[4], but at the same time she was described as withdrawn and uncouth. Both sides of her character were true. The testimony she gave for the Cause of Thérèse reveals not only her observation of Thérèse's heroic virtue, but a lot about herself as well. She said that when she entered Carmel she found the community in a very disappointing state. She had thought that all Carmelites were saints, but found in the Lisieux community that 'they were lacking in silence, regularity and especially mutual charity, and there were some lamentable divisions among them'[5]

Acknowledging that there were some very edifying nuns as well, she could see that Thérèse was in a class of her own; she observed her very closely, and said she never found the least imperfection in her. This was a problem for her; Madeleine expected the whole community to be saints, but when she found one who was, it was too much for her. Even though she acknowledged that Thérèse had all the qualities to train the novices, and was herself a living example of what she taught them, she found her novice mistress too perfect. This was the reason, she said, why she avoided her and refused to co-operate.

Thérèse herself did everything she could to win her trust, cheering her up when she was depressed, showing her any little kindness she could. Madeleine said that she esteemed Thérèse, but in her presence she simply clammed up through timidity. She was one of those who often felt as if Thérèse could see into her soul. Sadly, she was not able to tell Thérèse this, and Thérèse herself did not realise the problem. Was this because Thérèse, in her humility, was so acutely aware of her littleness and her imperfection that she was unaware that the example she set could be daunting to others?

One can have some sympathy with Madeleine; someone who is just too perfect could be a living reproach. Did Thérèse expect too much from her? Thérèse said that she would speak the truth, whatever it cost her, and that 'If you don't want to practice virtue, go back to the world'.[6] Madeleine gave an example of this total honesty in Thérèse who could not abide the slightest falsehood. Just for a joke, the novice tried to frighten Thérèse by pretending to see a big spider. 'She reproached me and told me that jocose lies did not become nuns, that one must always be "true"'.[7] Was this taking the absoluteness of truth a little too far, and did Madeleine feel rebuffed at this attempt to have an easier relationship with her novice mistress?

Madeleine had an experience of the depths of her novice mistress's love for God. She recounted how, one day she was in Thérèse's room when Thérèse 'said to me in a tone of voice that I cannot reproduce: "God is not loved enough! And yet he is so good and kind…

Oh, how I wish I could die!" And then she began to sob. Not understanding what it was to love God so vehemently, I looked on in amazement, and wondered what kind of an extraordinary creature I was standing in front of.'[8]

She also witnessed Thérèse's last moments. 'I saw with amazement how she raised her head again when she seemed to be dead and stared up with a look of amazement and extreme happiness. I have often been present at nun's deaths but I have never seen anything like that.'[9]

Thérèse was never able to win Madeleine's confidence during her life, but in September 1907, Madeleine was confined to the infirmary with ulcerated legs and boils which increased in seriousness over a period of eight months. Her leg was beginning to wither. In May the following year, Mother Marie-Ange, Prioress at the time, suggested that she pray to Thérèse for her intercession. The community made a novena, during which her leg became worse, but during a second novena she was completely cured. On the first Sunday of June Madeleine resumed her duties in the kitchen and never suffered a recurrence of the problem.

She also recalled an incident in the kitchen when, in the summer of 1910 she had to fill the boiler with four large pitchers of water, and another sister, Jeanne-Marie, offered to help her. They began by emptying the boiler completely. Madeleine returned with one pitcher which they emptied into the boiler, but when she returned with a second pitcher, they found to their amazement that the boiler was full of water. When Jeanne-Marie admitted that she felt very tired, and had prayed to Thérèse to help her, they had no doubt that she had. Thérèse would not have wanted that amelioration for herself if she had been in their place, but lovingly came to their aid to relieve their tiredness.

This was a turning point for Madeleine; perhaps this incident convinced her that Thérèse really did understand the struggles of others, and when she had spoken of her own weakness and littleness she really meant it. Madeleine now received healing not only of body but also of her entire character, such that even she was amazed. She had always been hard-working, and she served the community faithfully in the kitchen until her death 11 January 1916.

Many complain when God doesn't seem to answer prayer. Thérèse may have thought that God hadn't answered her prayers for her difficult novice during her life. However, in his own time and in his own way, God did indeed answer her prayers, and surely Thérèse was rejoicing in heaven that the straying sheep was now safely ensconced on the Good Shepherd's shoulders.

Sister Martha of Jesus

Of all the novices, Martha of Jesus was perhaps one of whom least was expected. Mother Agnès described her as 'a poor little unintelligent sister', and other sisters as foolish, tactless and bothersome. Thérèse, more charitably, saw her as innocent, frank, communicative and pure-hearted. It was true that she won over the little sister, who had entered three months before her, so that she could open herself totally to Thérèse, who was eight years younger than she.

Desirée Cauvin was born at Griverville 16 July 1865. She had had a hard life; both her parents had died when she was young, and she had spent most of her childhood and teenage years in various orphanages. This could explain some of her difficulties later on, since these factors had probably contributed to her unstable, emotionally unbalanced character, her sometimes violent temper, and especially her need for a mother-figure.

Her birthday falling on the Feast of Our Lady of Mount Carmel may explain her choice of Carmel as her vocation to the religious life, and she entered the Lisieux Carmel 23 December 1887 as a lay sister.

With her difficult character, moody and sullen, with violent mood swings and a ferocious temper, the community delayed her Clothing and she had a full year as a postulant rather than the customary six months. She eventually received the habit 2 May 1889, and was professed 23 September 1890. From the very beginning she recognised in Thérèse someone who was special and soon attached herself to her fellow novice. With her, Thérèse had the advantage that Martha recognised her faults and really wanted to overcome them and become a holy Carmelite. Thérèse had to start at the beginning with her and shared practices such as making a list of her 'conquests' and acts of virtue on beads, which Thérèse herself had long grown out of. She also changed the time of her annual retreat each year to fit in with Martha's, so that they could come together for the recreation periods, when Thérèse would help her by her teaching and encouragement. She wrote out prayers for her, and Martha was so helped by Thérèse that she received permission to stay in the Novitiate when she would normally have progressed into the full community, so that she could continue to benefit from the younger nun's teaching.

There was one area in her young charge's development that caused Thérèse great concern. Lacking a mother for most of her life, when Martha entered

Carmel she developed an unhealthy attachment to Mother Marie de Gonzague, who didn't help but instead encouraged her affection. Since she had had the same temptation herself Thérèse could sympathise and understand Martha's attachment; she could understand Martha's desire to see in Marie de Gonzague the mother she had never had, but she also recognised that in a small community such attachments could be unhealthy, both for Martha and also for the Prioress.

Thérèse bided her time until 8 December 1892, when she felt this was the time when she had to speak out. She was only too well aware of the dangers—Martha might resent her interference, given the strength of her attachment and her need for a mother figure, and explode in anger. Since Mother Marie de Gonzague encouraged such attachment, she might incur the Prioress's wrath at her interference and seriously thought she might even be sent away from the convent. In the event, Martha was given the light to see for herself the truth of what Thérèse was saying. Thérèse held Martha in her arms, both in tears, but the task was done. It was to the credit of both of them that Martha never had a similar unhealthy attachment to her young novice mistress.

It was Martha who often served up Thérèse with the almost inedible leftovers that none of the other sisters would eat, and yet on the other hand would invite her into the kitchen to warm up when she was becoming ill, an indulgence that Thérèse refused. Her attitude towards Thérèse varied from admiration, to fear of the young mistress's high standards. When she sometimes became upset by the corrections, she would sulk and refuse to speak to Thérèse for a while, but on the other hand she treasured her teaching highly.

She might have been simple, but she also made the point, when giving her testimony for the Cause of Thérèse's canonisation, that those in the Novitiate were able to observe Thérèse's heroic virtue at close quarters. Many in the community saw her only as a devout nun, she said, observant, but nothing out of the ordinary. As one nun remarked, Thérèse had never suffered! But Martha could see her humility, her love of poverty—she regretted later on that she had burnt Thérèse's alpargates after her death, because they would have been an eloquent testimony to her love of poverty—the way she mortified herself in little ways, such as not leaning against the wall in the refectory, even when she was so exhausted she could hardly stand.

Gradually, in the years before her death, Martha's character changed completely. She underwent a spiritual transformation during the sufferings of her final months, when Thérèse's Little Way took root in her and gave her the victory over her faults that she had battled so long to overcome. She died 4 September 1916.

Notes

1 Thérèse of Lisieux, *Story of a Soul* (Washington DC: ICS Publications, 1976), translated by J. Clarke OCD, pp. 238ff.
2 J.-F. Six, *Light of the Night* (London: SCM Press Ltd, 1996), p. 94.
3 C. O'Mahoney OCD (ed.), *St Therese of Lisieux by Those Who Knew Her* (Dublin: Veritas Publications, 1975), p. 261.
4 G. Gaucher, *The Passion of Thérèse of Lisieux* (Victoria: St Paul Publications, 1989), p. 28.
5 O'Mahoney, *Those Who Knew Her,* p. 260.
6 *Ibid.*
7 *Ibid.,* p. 262.
8 *Ibid.,* p. 261.
9 *Ibid.,* p. 264.

9

SISTER MARIE OF THE TRINITY

When Marie-Louise Castel entered the Lisieux Carmel 16 June 1894, Thérèse found in her someone who would become a true friend and above all a disciple who was eager to absorb all the spiritual teaching that Thérèse could give her. The friendship that developed between the two perhaps lifts a veil over another suffering that Thérèse endured during her first years in Carmel. She was of course much younger than the other sisters there; two companions in the Novitiate were uncongenial, one was the 48 year old Sister Marie Philomène, 'very holy and very limited', and the truculent Sister Martha. Thérèse deliberately cut herself off from the consolation she could have had from her two elder sisters, even from Marie of the Sacred Heart who was still in the Novitiate. There was no-one with whom she could share her growing sense of the way in which the Lord was guiding her in the ways of confidence and abandonment to the merciful love of God, in a Carmel where this was not the accepted religious outlook.

Taking at first the name of Marie-Agnès of the Holy Face, Mother Marie of the Angels described the little streetwise Parisian as 'The rogue of Carmel! Never feels embarrassed by anything and knows perfectly how to pull herself out of any affair'. Despite their different backgrounds and a somewhat rough character which Thérèse would at first find disconcerting, they had much in common. They both came from a strong Catholic and family background. Marie-Louise was born in a village in Calvados, 12 August 1874, the seventh surviving child, with eight babies who had died. Like Thérèse, she spent her first years with a wet nurse, a maternal aunt, and returned to her family when she was four years old. Her father was a school master, but after the atheistic Government of the day secularised all schools in 1882, he was forced to resign for insisting on saying morning prayers with his students. They moved to Paris when Marie-Louise was eight, and her father became a merchant.

It was a fervent household, and Marie-Louise was drawn especially to devotion to the Holy Face. Her father had set aside a room as an oratory, where a lamp burned day and night before an icon of the Holy Face. In such an atmosphere, the young girl was drawn early on to a desire for the religious life, and at the age of twelve, after praying a novena, felt drawn to the Carmelites. She was impatient to put her desire into practice and entered the Paris Carmel on l'avenue de Messine 30 April 1891 when she was sixteen years old, and was given the name of Agnès of Jesus. However, her health suffered, and she left in July 1893.

Her father took her to Trouville to recuperate and later that month she was well enough to visit the Carmel at Lisieux. Because of the close links between the two Carmels Thérèse had already heard of the little novice, and had remarked, 'If they had to send me away, I know very well what I would do: I would go and find little Sister Agnès of Jesus and we would live together until we had reached the age to re-enter Carmel!'[1] Already, bonds were being forged between the two young women. For her part, Marie was looking forward to meeting the young Carmelite who, she had been told, had entered Carmel at only fifteen.

Marie-Louise's desire for Carmel was undiminished, and she was dismayed that, because of a proposed change in the law, her Paris Carmel would not accept her back until she was 21. She therefore turned to the Lisieux Carmel and met with the same resistance from Canon Delatroëtte as Thérèse had done. Once again, though, as in Thérèse's case, he changed his mind, and she entered 16 June 1894. Thérèse, delighted that she was no longer the youngest sister in the community, was appointed as her 'angel'. Mother Agnès, though, had already given her the task of being more of a mentor to the young Novitiate sisters, so she became, in effect, the postulant's Novice Mistress.

A month later, Thérèse wrote to Céline, who wanted news of the new postulant, giving her impression of her charge:

> You want to know some news of my girl. Well, I think she WILL STAY; she was not brought up like us; it is very unfortunate for her, her education is the cause of her unattractive ways, but basically she is good. Now she loves me, but I am careful to touch her only with white silk gloves.[2]

Marie was at first given the name Marie-Agnès of the Holy Face but it was later changed to Marie of the Trinity and the Holy Face because it was causing confusion, since in the Normandy dialect it sounded very much like Mère Agnès. To Marie, this was providential, and she told Thérèse of an incident in her home that had occurred a few years back, when a crystal glass lamp before the image of the Holy Face turned black. Her father had wiped it clean, but a small brown triangle remained and could not be erased. Thérèse was quick to see the symbolism, and wrote to Marie that her trials were slowly clearing the darkness from her, leaving her with the mark of the Trinity.

Marie herself recognised she wasn't natural material for the religious life. Despite her two years in the Paris Carmel, she found it hard, with her lively and impetuous character, to conform to Carmelite life, and many of the sisters found her difficult and unruly. She was naturally inquisitive and interested in what was going on around her, so her novice mistress had to help her learn the religious custom of 'custody of the eyes'. This was the raw material on which Thérèse would work, not necessarily the stuff of which great saints would be made. But this was exactly Thérèse's point. Everyone is created for heaven, everyone is called to holiness, whatever their character, and since it is God, in Jesus, who works the transformation, then all they need to do is surrender themselves totally to him and allow his holiness to penetrate, heal and transform them into the person he wills them to be.

Marie of the Trinity, in particular, with her quick mind and willingness to question and explore, was a catalyst for Thérèse to formulate and explain her Little Way; it encouraged her to devise novel and imaginative ways to get her message across to her young charges. Marie will always be remembered for two ways in which Thérèse gave tangible aids to help her. Her novice cried easily, so Thérèse humorously gave her one of the shells she used in her painting, so that when she was tempted to cry she should collect her tears in the shell. Not that she had a lachrymose temperament: in the photographs taken of the community, her lips are always turned up in a smile, and in one of them, at a time when subjects had to remain still during the exposure and therefore have a solemn face, she is breaking out in a smile.

Then, one Christmas, Thérèse had included a top for her in the presents under the tree, and Marie quickly showed the community how it was used. One day, during Thérèse's illness, her young novice confessed that she needed some distraction and to let off some of her energy. Understanding her character, Thérèse told her to retrieve the top from the Novitiate attic and have a good play with it. Marie always retained that childlike, energetic and playful character. When the family had lived in Paris she loved exploring the shops, the street shows and markets. The last thing she did before entering Lisieux Carmel was to take a ride on the merry-go-round at the fair there.

Despite her difficulties in adapting to religious life, and occasional doubts about her vocation, the young novice was soon won over to Thérèse's teaching and developed rapidly in the spiritual life. If she became dispirited at her lack of progress, Thérèse would laughingly say to her, 'so, you have no vocation', reminding her of the occasion when Marie came to her with just that conclusion. Thérèse, moreover, recognised that despite her faults, Marie had a generous character. She also had a beautiful voice, and Thérèse said that in Choir it made up for her own thin and toneless voice, made all the more difficult as she was already suffering from hoarseness and cough, the first sign of her tuberculosis.

On the Feast of the Holy Trinity, 11 June 1895, Thérèse had composed her famous Offering to Merciful Love. Marie of the Trinity should have made her Profession at the end of that year, but Mother Marie de Gonzague felt that she was not ready for such a step, and also wanted to receive her vows when she expected to be re-elected as Prioress. In her disappointment, Thérèse showed her the prayer she had composed, and suggested that Marie should also make the Offering to Merciful Love. At first Marie was reluctant, feeling it was far beyond her, but eventually agreed and on the first Sunday of Advent pronounced her Act of Oblation before the Blessed Sacrament. She felt herself flooded with graces, and all that day experienced the tangible presence of the Eucharistic Jesus within her. She was then so enthusiastic about the Prayer that she wanted to make copies to send to her friends and relations, but Thérèse warned her against it. For Thérèse, the Prayer was not a pious devotion to be added to a list of prayers, but a commitment of one's whole life and being, not to be taken lightly. Finally, on 30 April 1896, Marie pronounced her vows.

Marie of the Trinity often became discouraged at her failings, but for Thérèse, failings were an indispensable part of the Little Way:

> You are complaining about something that should cause you the greatest happiness. Where would your merit be, if you could fight only when you feel courage? What does it matter if you have none, provided that you act as if you do! When you feel too weak to pick up a ball of yarn and you do it anyway for the love of Jesus, you have more merit than if you had accomplished something more important in a moment of fervour. Instead of feeling sad when you feel your weakness, rejoice that God is providing you with the opportunity to save a greater number of souls for him![3]

The relationship between the two young women deepened from that of novice and mistress into a deep and affectionate friendship. One day, during evening recreation, Thérèse came in, burning with fever, and sat down on her heels beside Marie. She felt so ill that it would be impossible for her to hold a conversation, so she whispered to Marie, 'I am coming next to you so that you can guard me. I feel I no longer have the strength to carry on a conversation; you should look as if you are talking to me so that others won't start to speak to me.'[4] Marie was the only one at that time to whom she confessed her extreme weakness.

Thérèse sometimes dreamt of her novice and told her, 'You must see how much I love you, since even in my dreams I think about you!' adding, 'I can't tell you that I love you more today than I did yesterday, because my love for you has become so intense that it cannot increase!'[5]

Not that Thérèse saved Marie, her 'doll' as she called her, from corrections and hard lessons. One day Marie came to her complaining that she had been overlooked at the meal and had not had the dessert. Thérèse told her that, as her penance for not accepting this small deprivation for the love of God, she must go to the kitchen and ask the sisters for her portion, something that Marie recoiled from, from embarrassment. Thérèse, though, was adamant, giving Marie a lesson she would not forget.

It was a great sadness and deprivation to both of them, then, when, in the Spring of 1897 Thérèse's health deteriorated to such an extent that she was installed permanently in the infirmary. Marie was the assistant infirmarian, but to save her from possible infection, Mother Marie de Gonzague removed her from the post. She was now able to see Thérèse only occasionally, but she had a wealth of teaching to draw upon. Indeed, after Thérèse's death she felt her presence even more, guiding and instructing her in the way of confidence, littleness and joyful surrender to the love of God.

After Thérèse's death life in the Carmel changed radically as her fame began to spread. Marie of the Trinity was a great copyist. She filled eleven notebooks with writings from the spiritual masters; extracts from St John Chrysostom alone were 442 pages long. She also copied out a unified Gospel, 293 pages long, in beautiful calligraphy, for Mother Agnès' feast day. When letters began to pour in to the Carmel following the publication of 'Story of a Soul', she was the obvious choice to become one of the team of 'writers' as they were nicknamed, who replied to them.

There is a little remarked aspect to Thérèse's spirituality, that of spiritual motherhood, and it was one that she passed on to Marie. All her sacrifices, her prayer, her sufferings were what Thérèse termed 'earning her living' for her spiritual children, as she called the souls she longed to save. Seeing Marie sauntering along to the laundry on a Wash Day, admiring the flowers, Thérèse overtook her remarking, 'Is this how one hurries when one has children to feed and has to work to keep them alive?'[6] This spiritual motherhood is basic to Carmelite spirituality, and, indeed, of every form of contemplative and prayer life. It is the charism of every Christian to 'bring forth' Christ in a spiritual manner by their life in Christ, as Mary brought forth Christ in her flesh.

After her novice mistress' death, Marie had the joy of putting that spiritual motherhood into practice in a very direct way. Her father had become very much involved in the work of Fr Roussel, who had begun 'The Work for Apprentices' for the poor children in Paris. A new director of the movement, Fr Daniel Brottier, wanted to build a chapel for them, dedicated to Saint Thérèse, and was delighted to discover that Marie was Victor Castel's daughter, and furthermore, had been a novice of Thérèse herself. When the Archbishop of the diocese, Mgr Dubois, heard that he wanted to dedicate the chapel to Saint Thérèse, he remarked that it would have been more appropriate, since it was for young boys, to dedicate it to a young male saint such as Aloysius Gonzaga or Stanislaus Koska.

'You are right, of course,' was Fr Brottier's reply, 'but it seems to me that the children who don't have mothers are in even greater need of a little mama!'

Marie, too, by her prayer and sacrificial life, also became 'a little mama' to the boys, a work that was wholeheartedly supported by the Lisieux Carmel as a whole.

Marie was named 'of the Trinity', but she also kept the title 'and of the Holy Face'. In February 1923, when she was 38 years old, this devotion took on a tragic poignancy. She contracted pneumonia and shortly afterwards a tubercular growth appeared on the back of her head. It was lupus, a cancerous growth that gradually spread over her whole face. During the last eight years of her life she described herself as a leper, and wore a veil to cover the ravaged part of her face. Towards the end, it took two hours a day to change the dressings.

It was during this time that her practice of the Little Way was put to its greatest and most triumphant test. Above all, it was Thérèse's spirituality of the smile that characterised her. Years before, she had told Thérèse that rather than crying in public, she would save her tears for the Lord.

'Keep yourself absolutely from doing any such thing!' was Thérèse's vigorous response. 'You should appear even less sad in front of him than in front of creatures ... Jesus loves happy hearts. He loves a soul that is always smiling. When, then, will you know how to hide your pain from him, or to tell him singing that you are happy to suffer for him?'[7]

This was a lesson that Marie took fully to heart, and put into practice in the most harrowing of circumstances. The pain and suffering of her increasingly leprous face meant that she walked a hard Calvary which she embraced with a deep and unshakeable peace. Her body became so bent that she could walk only with the help of a cane. She described it in words reminiscent of Saint Thérèse:

> I feel only my misery and powerlessness, I see only darkness yet, in spite of everything, I remain in an inexpressible peace. Jesus sleeps: Mary, too. I don't seek to wake them, and like Thérèse I peacefully await the shores of heaven.[8]

Sometimes that inner peace became a foretaste of the joys of heaven:

'It is a peace so delicious that I could truly sing from morning until night,' she wrote to Mother Agnès. 'It is not a passing peace, but the possession of an enduring joy that makes me want to say about everything that happens to me, the happy and the painful things: 'You overwhelm me with joy, O Lord, by everything you do.'[9]

This was only one of many notes she wrote to her Prioress, who became a true mother to her, encouraging her on her painful yet indescribably beautiful spiritual journey, during which their relationship became ever closer and more loving.

Her joy that she spoke of so often was visible on that part of her face that could be seen, as Fr Philip of the Trinity, a Carmelite who visited her in 1940, bore witness:

> She was already more than sixty-five years old, but carried her years courageously despite the lupus that she suffered in half of her face (covered by a white veil). She gave me an impression of holiness and simplicity that I will never forget. She spoke to me about St Thérèse with an affectionate and respectful veneration that still moves me. I also remember her half-veiled face bathed in a wholly spiritual light.[10]

Despite her suffering, she considered that even here on earth she could taste an anticipation of heaven; her one desire was to love God like Thérèse loved him, to be the joy of his heart as she had been.

Her ordeal was to last another four years. At the beginning of 1944 the community was hit by a flu epidemic, and Marie of the Trinity, in her precarious state of health, was fatally affected. She received the last sacraments 15 January, and the following day she gently breathed her last. Her final words were, 'In heaven I will follow little Thérèse everywhere!'

As a young girl her dream was to have a friend who was also a saint. The Lord fulfilled that dream abundantly, and in her turn Marie of the Trinity did not let her friend down. The Little Way of Saint Thérèse had brought her surely and triumphantly to the holiness for which she was created and for which she had yearned.

Notes

1 P. Descouvemont, *Thérèse of Lisieux and Marie of the Trinity* (New York: St Paul Publications (Alba House), 1993), p. 7.
2 Thérèse of Lisieux, *Letters Vol 11.* (Washington DC: ICS Publications, 1988), translated by J. Clarke OCD, p. 872.
3 Descouvemont, *Marie of the Trinity*, p. 104.
4 *Ibid.*, p. 35.
5 *Ibid.*, p. 34.
6 *Ibid.*, p. 104.
7 *Ibid.*, p. 72.
8 *Ibid.*, p. 118.
9 *Ibid.*, p. 1225.
10 *Ibid.*, p. 143, note 11.

10

SISTER MARIE OF THE EUCHARIST

MARIE GUÉRIN

WHEN THEIR BELOVED mother died, it was the Guérins who became invaluable to the bereaved Martin family. Even before that, Marie, their younger daughter and two and a half years older than Thérèse, became even greater friends with her during their time together at the Benedictine Abbey where they were semi-boarders. Unaccustomed to the rougher ways of the girls she met there, Thérèse found herself like a fish out of water, but Marie shared Thérèse's gentler taste in games. Their favourite game consisted in pretending to be hermits, which they played on their days off on Thursdays. They built a tiny hermitage in which one would pray while the other tended a little vegetable patch. Thérèse described humorously how, one day, wanting to preserve their prayerfulness and with neither of them willing to be the one to keep their eyes open to guide the other, they both kept their eyes closed and ran into a greengrocer's display, much to the owner's annoyance.

At this time Marie, as the young Thérèse noticed, was a spoilt and sickly little girl, always ailing, who often whimpered to gain attention. Her mother would then baby her, and Thérèse, who also suffered from almost daily headaches, decided she, too, wanted the same cosseting. 'So one evening, sitting in an armchair,' Thérèse records, she set about crying herself. However, because she normally bore her headaches without complaint, she received no sympathy but only a scolding.

This assessment of Marie was also shared by Céline when was staying with the Guérins at La Musse. She wrote to Thérèse in Carmel that 'I am living the life of the exiled here. It's true I have Marie, who is very loving and devoted to me, but I feel that her soul has not been matured through suffering. At times I find her a little too childish and not sufficiently submissive to sacrifice'.[1]

However, Marie had great potential. Those childhood games of being a hermit were not completely play for her, and in a letter to Thérèse, now in Carmel, Marie described her desire for solitude, not easy to find in the Guérin household while they were preparing for her elder sister Jeanne's wedding to a young doctor, François le Néele: 'While Jeanne's fiancé is here, the means of union with God are difficult to carry out, so meditation is often set aside', she wrote. Troubled with bad thoughts, every moment a struggle, no joy in receiving communion, yet 'Meditation, however, is a moment of delight for me; I could spend days in this exercise… I love to breathe in an air that is purer than the air of this earth.'

She doesn't feel as if she is benefiting from it, though, and while in her meditation she is burning with love, 'once I return to the combat, fortitude abandons me.'[2] She felt that she had wasted twenty years of her life, with nothing to show for it. She turned to Thérèse as one who had much fervour in God's service, and wanted her friend to teach her how to walk in it with courage in the same way as she did.

Thérèse's response is to rebut her cousin's glowing opinion of her: 'You are mistaken, my darling, if you believe that your little Thérèse always walks with fervour on the road to virtue'.[3] Thérèse considers herself weak, very weak, but that is precisely the lesson the Lord is teaching her, to rejoice in that very weakness. So she counsels Marie to embrace her poverty and weakness, and to 'thank God for all the graces He is giving you, and don't be so *ungrateful* as not to acknowledge them.'[4]

It is unsurprising that Marie also began to discern a vocation to Carmel, and she entered the Lisieux Carmel on the Feast of the Assumption, 15 August 1895. The young cousin she had played with in the world was now her novice mistress in all but name. It was not easy for her, now twenty five and accustomed to her independence, to take instruction from the younger woman, especially as she had become close to the Prioress; Mother de Gonzague had directed her before her entry and was officially her novice mistress now. Gradually, though, she began to admire and respect her younger cousin.

She was given the name of Marie of the Eucharist, which acknowledged her great love for the Sacrament. Marie suffered for many years from scruples and even, at one time, during a trip to Paris and affected by the sights she saw there, felt she should deprive herself from receiving Holy Communion. Thérèse immediately wrote back assuring her that she understood, because for years she herself had also suffered from scruples. However,

> You haven't committed the *shadow of any evil!*… this is doing just what the devil wants … he wants to deprive Jesus of a loved sanctuary…

> Dear little sister, *receive Communion often,* very often… That is the *only remedy* if you want to be healed, and Jesus hasn't placed this attraction in your soul for nothing.'[5]

This letter encouraged Marie, but it had an even more far-reaching effect. In it, Thérèse describes how strongly she feels about the effects of receiving Holy Communion has on the one who receives It, and the harm that comes from not receiving the Sacrament through scruples:

> The evil one knows well that he can't make a soul that wants to belong totally to Jesus to commit a sin, so he tries to make the soul believe that it has. It is already much for him to put disturbance in the soul, but to satisfy his rage something else is needed; he wants to deprive Jesus of a loved tabernacle, and, not being able to enter this sanctuary, he wants, at least, that it remain *empty* and without any Master!… Alas, what will become of this poor heart?…When the devil has succeeded in drawing the soul away from Holy Communion, he *has won everything*… And Jesus weeps![6]

On 29 October 1910, Monseigneur de Teil, the Postulator of the cause for Thérèse's beatification and canonisation, showed this letter to Pope Pius X, who was already a strong advocate of frequent communion. On reading this letter, with its explanation of the value of receiving communion to the Christian life, replied, 'We must hurry this cause'. He saw in the young Carmelite one who would be invaluable in promoting frequent and reverent reception of communion, with her sound teaching on its benefits.

The Community were delighted with their new postulant. Thérèse wrote to Jeanne, now Mme La Néele, that

> It is a great consolation for me, the *old* senior of the novitiate, to see so much gaiety surrounding my last days; it rejuvenates me and, in spite of my seven and a half years of religious life, my gravity often breaks down in the presence of the charming rascal who delights the whole Community.[7]

She was also delighted that she had in Marie yet another one who had a beautiful singing voice. As novice mistress, Thérèse noted in the same letter how Marie had grown spiritually: 'Her beautiful voice is the joy and delight of our recreations, but what delights my heart especially, more than our dear angel's talents and exterior qualities, is her disposition to virtue.'

The Community soon made use of her beautiful voice and talents; she composed songs that they would sing as they bent over the tubs scrubbing the laundry, to relieve the tedium of the arduous task. Still, Thérèse felt she needed to tone down Marie's exuberance at recreation somewhat, and Marie jotted down her counsels:

> In recreation, practice virtue, be lovable towards all, no matter with whom you are speaking; be happy out of virtue not whim. When you are sad, forget yourself and show cheerfulness… Take pleasure, but especially out of love for others… There is a foolish gaiety about you at times, do you believe it pleases the Sisters?… They laugh at your foolishness, it is true, but it does not edify them.[8]

Marie was delighted that, soon after she received the habit 17 March 1896, she was assigned to help in the sacristy, and it was as sacristan that the famous incident occurred that made such an impression on Thérèse:

Marie wanted to light the candles for a procession but she had no matches; however, seeing a little lamp which was burning in front of some relics, she approached it. Alas, it was half out; there remained only a feeble glimmer on its blackened wick. She succeeded in lighting her candle from it, and with this candle, she lighted those of the whole community.

'It is the same with the Communion of Saints', Thérèse reflected. 'Very often, without our knowing it, the graces and lights that we receive are due to a hidden soul, for God wills that the saints communicate grace to each other through prayer with great love.'[9]

As Thérèse's illness progressed, being the daughter of a pharmacist and sister-in-law to a doctor, Marie was able to keep the concerned Guérins up to date with news of their dearly loved niece. To this end Mother de Gonzague gave her unlimited access to Thérèse in the infirmary. She described to her family in detail the progress of Thérèse's illness, but also told them of the happiness and the sense of fun that never deserted her. 'If you were to see our little patient', she wrote to them, 'you wouldn't be able to stop laughing. She has to be always saying something funny. Ever since she has become convinced that she is going to die, she has been gay as a little finch.'[10] However, even when seriously ill, Thérèse continued to train her novice in even the smallest things, at one time telling her not to sit sideways on the chair during a visit.

Thérèse saw in Marie of the Eucharist a twin soul, one who would be her substitute after her death, and not only for her singing. Marie herself understood the deep bond between them, writing to her sister Jeanne,

> It's true that the older ones [her sisters Marie and Pauline] could call themselves our mothers, but we two, the two little ones, we formed one, we had never left each other, our souls, our hearts were beating in unison... When my dear Thérèse has died, I shall try to offer to the Lord a song which I haven't sung as yet; the bitterness of this suffering will provide me with a new voice.[11]

One day Thérèse looked at her 'with such a profound gaze that I'll never forget it', Marie wrote to her father, and Thérèse said, 'Oh, little Sister, promise me you'll become a saint, a great saint.' When I looked at her in amazement, she continued: 'Yes, and if I say this to you, it's because I find in you all that is necessary for this... When I'm no longer on earth, you'll have to be a saint for two, in order that God lose nothing; I feel that your soul is being called to the same type of perfection as my own, and you must replace me when I'm gone.'[12]

Marie well understood the 'type of perfection' to which she was called, describing Thérèse in a letter to a cousin:

> Hers is not an extraordinary sanctity; there is no love of extraordinary penances, no, only love for God. People in the world can imitate her sanctity, for she has tried only to do everything through love and to accept all little contradictions, all little sacrifices that come at each moment as coming from God's hands. She saw God in everything, and she carried out all her

> actions as perfectly as possible. Daily duty came before everything else.[13]

Marie promised her that she would be a saint when Thérèse had left for heaven. 'At that moment, I'll put my whole heart into it.' 'Oh, don't wait for that', was Thérèse's reply. 'Begin now… Believe me, don't wait until tomorrow to begin becoming a saint.'

Sadly, Marie did become Thérèse's substitute after her death by contracting the same disease as her, perhaps due to the close contact she had had with Thérèse during her illness. Marie of the Trinity recounted a dream she had had September 1904, six months before Marie's death:

> We started a novena to Sr Thérèse to obtain the healing of her cousin. During the following night I dreamed that the cousin said in agony to Mother Agnès: 'Don't be sad. If you hear Thérèse's voice after my death, this will be a sign that I went straight to heaven.' In fact, immediately after her death I saw her quite nimbly and rapidly crossing the tree-lined path of a beautiful garden. Then I heard Thérèse's voice saying to us: 'Rejoice, all of you, she is happy with me forever in heaven'… Thérèse made [me] to understand that on earth, Sr Marie of the Eucharist often feared that God rejected her; it seemed to her that she did nothing and that all her suffering was useless. But it was this very condition that gave her all her merit and that purified her. The imperfections for which she could be reproached had not prevented her from going straight to heaven. Unknown to her, her failings were made up for through the painful privation of spiritual consolations.[14]

Marie's life could be seen as another message of Thérèse's Little Way: that faults, failings and imperfections are not a bar to heaven, but can be the way of humility and trust in the merciful love of God. Marie of the Eucharist died 14 April 1905.

Notes

1 Thérèse of Lisieux, *Letters Vol 1.* (Washington DC: ICS Publications, 1982), translated by J. Clarke OCD p. 627.
2 *Ibid.,* p. 638.
3 *Ibid.,* p. 641.
4 *Ibid.,* p. 640.
5 *Ibid.,* pp. 567ff.
6 *Ibid.*
7 *Ibid.,* p. 915.
8 *Ibid.,* note 5.
9 P. Martin, (Mother Agnès of Jesus), *St Thérèse of Lisieux, Her Last Conversations* (Washington DC: ICS Publications 1977), translated by J. Clarke OCD, p. 99.
10 *Ibid.,* p. 274.
11 *Ibid.,* p. 278.
12 *Ibid.,* p. 250.
13 *Ibid.*
14 P. Descouvemont, *Thérèse of Lisieux and Marie of the Trinity* (New York: St Paul Publications (Alba House), 1993), p. 52.

11

SOME SISTERS IN THE COMMUNITY

THÉRÈSE SAID THAT when she entered the Lisieux Carmel, the life held no surprises for her. How true was this? She expected an austere life, with many trials and sacrifices. But she came from a family that was warm and loving, even though the sisters were so disparate in their characters and there were some disagreements. It could be true to say that she had rarely met malice, jealousy, spitefulness, except at school. So was she aware beforehand of the various and often difficult characters of the sisters in the Community? Did she expect everyone to be saints? She did indeed have the privilege of knowing Mother Geneviève, who was saintly by any standard, and she said that Mother Marie of the Angels, despite her shortcomings 'was a real saint', but many of the sisters did not live up to these standards.

What is remarkable about Thérèse's introduction to a very dysfunctional community was the way in which she embraced all of them and put love of them at the heart of her striving for holiness. After all, it was only a few short years since her time at the Benedictine Abbey school, when she was so timid that she was unable to cope with the roughness of some of the girls there. Now, she had to cope with the barbs and shafts of unkind words and criticism, which she admitted did hurt her. She was not blind to the sisters' shortcomings, writing:

> Of course, one does not have enemies in Carmel, but still there are natural attractions, one feels drawn to a certain sister, whereas you go a long way round to avoid meeting another.
>
> The lack of judgment, education, the touchiness of some characters, all these things do not make life very pleasant. I know very well that these moral weaknesses are chronic, that there is no hope of a cure.[1]

'Those around me are really good, but there is something,' she admitted, 'I don't know what, that repels me.'[2] She lived in a desert of unloving, in the confined milieu of an enclosed community, where she had to face her problems without the distractions found in the world outside. Now, this young girl of fifteen began, with amazing maturity, to explore the true meaning of love of neighbour in the light of her love for God, in the context of the many difficult characters she met with in her sisters. To paraphrase the words of Saint John of the Cross, where there was no love she put love and drew forth love.

There was Sister Aimée of Jesus, from Lisieux, who entered the Carmel 13 October 1871, received the habit 19 March 1872 and was professed 8 May 1873. Strong, active and capable, she had no patience with artistic temperaments and was one of those who formed the faction opposed to the Martin sisters. She considered three Martin sisters, with their artistic gifts, at least one too many, and strongly resisted Céline's entry after her father's death. She was so opposed that Thérèse asked God to give her a sign: if Aimée withdrew her opposition, then she would take it as a sign that her father was now in heaven. The sister suddenly accepted Céline, and the way was open for her entry into the community.

Under her rough and gruff exterior, though, Aimée had a really generous heart.[3] When Thérèse was too ill to move herself Aimée would lift her in her strong arms while her bed was remade. She never forgot the radiant smile of gratitude with which Thérèse rewarded her.

Aimée admitted that she was one of the instruments God used to sanctify Thérèse, recognising that '[t]he charitable way she bore with my defects brought her to an outstanding degree of holiness'. Although she was not particularly intimate with her, Aimée was able to appreciate Thérèse's qualities. In her opinion, she would have made an excellent Prioress; 'she would have always acted prudently and charitably, and never abused her authority', she said, the last comment perhaps a barbed reference to Mother Marie de Gonzague's abuse of authority.

Many of the sisters were ill-disposed to Thérèse from the beginning, especially among the lay sisters, who did the heavy work of the monastery. They found Thérèse was slow and clumsy at manual work, which she had never done before. Sister Vincent de Paul, one of the lay sisters, described as very intelligent but somewhat eccentric, who hid a kind heart under a very rough exterior[4], had a sharp manner, called her the 'grand lady', 'the big clumsy goat' and Sister Snail', biting remarks made within Thérèse's hearing. She was an accomplished embroideress, but Thérèse found needlework very difficult, which was another black mark against her. Even as a small child Thérèse could be found reduced to tears as she hunched over her cobbled attempts at sewing.

Thérèse rewarded her after her death by healing her of cerebral anaemia, when, as her body was laid out in the choir, the sister came to kiss her feet. No-one is completely without their good points. Sister Saint Vincent was noted in the community for the long hours she spent before the Blessed Sacrament.

Thérèse was considered slow because she persevered in walking deliberately and prayerfully, so that even under her black veil the gardener could recognise her by her walk. One day, seeing her going to the laundry, Sister Saint Vincent remarked in annoyance: 'Look at her; she is in no hurry; when will she ever start the washing; she's good for nothing.'[5] Thérèse's deliberate walk was not lack of enthusiasm for the tiring work ahead, because she always took the least comfortable place in the laundry. Called Sister Amen for always arriving last, she never wanted to be flustered or brought out of her habitual sense of the presence of God and her sense of being a religious, with all that meant of a religious deportment. Because she always stopped whatever she was doing at the first sound of the bell—there is a letter of hers which shows that she stopped in the middle of a word she was writing—she was nevertheless always in time for the next religious exercise.

There were other pinpricks that tried her charity. As a postulant, she volunteered to take the elderly Sister St Pierre to the refectory after prayer time, which was a process that Thérèse described with some humour, but would be trying to anyone's patience. According to Sister St Pierre, she was walking her either too fast or too slow, not supporting her enough, not seating her properly when arriving in the refectory, not folding her sleeves back properly...[6] Nevertheless,

Thérèse was able to win her over, and what the elderly sister appreciated most was the radiant smile Thérèse gave her as she left.

In Choir, during prayer time, her nerves were so frayed that Thérèse sweated with the effort of listening to Sister Marie of Jesus, who had the strange habit of clicking her teeth, which in her autobiography was softened to clicking her rosary. She overcame this by pretending it was the sweetest of music. When she was assigned to help the portress Sister Raphael of the Heart of Mary at the turn, she had to practice the utmost patience in dealing with the Sister's difficult character; she admitted that sometimes, like a coward, she had to escape from situations for a while to regain her composure.

Later on, when Thérèse was given the work of painting the chapel with artwork, many of the sisters felt that she was not pulling her weight in the work of the monastery. Thérèse learnt to greet all these criticisms with a smile, and then she would seek out the sisters who had hurt her most, who she found most difficult, to sit with them at recreation and entertain them as only she could. Mother Marie of the Angels described her as, 'A mystic, a comedienne, she was everything. She knew how to make you weep with devotion and just as easily make you burst with laughter at recreation.'[7] With her great gift for mimicry, if she was not at recreation the sisters knew it would not be so entertaining. Thérèse had no time for 'sad saints', and instilled into her novices that they should go to recreation in order to give pleasure to their sisters.

A letter she wrote to Mother Agnès[8] describes an incident with another difficult sister, Sister St John the

Baptist. This sister impressed with her noble bearing, but to Thérèse she represented 'God's *severity*'. At one time she was in charge of the Linen Room, only a few yards away from Thérèse's cell, so she was in a good position to watch the comings and goings of the novices. In the Novitiate Sister Genevieve said that their hearts all beat a bit faster when they saw her coming; they were indignant at the demands she put on Thérèse, but impressed by their young novice mistress's calmness under provocation.

This day in May 1897, though, when Thérèse was with Mother Agnès and feeling very tired and feverish, even her sweetness was tested to the limit. Sister St John came to ask her help with some painting and refused to take no for an answer, even though Mother Agnès tried to intervene and point out how ill her sister was. Thérèse showed by a momentary expression the stress this put her under, but was reduced to tears of remorse and gratitude when the sister came to her a little later and apologised; Thérèse felt she deserved only God's 'severity' for this momentary lapse in her habitual readiness to help.

As we have seen, she deliberately sought out the company of those who were least agreeable to be with, and whom the rest of the community tried to avoid as much as possible.

One of these was Sister Thérèse of St Augustine. Born Julie Leroyer at Cressonnière (Calvados), she entered Carmel 1 May 1875, was clothed with the habit 15 October the same year, and was Professed 1 May 1877. Thérèse wrote in her autobiography that she had a natural antipathy towards the sister but set herself to win her over. 'There is in the Community a Sister who has the faculty of displeasing me in everything', she wrote; 'in her ways, her words, her character, everything seems very disagreeable to me.'[9] She therefore set out to do for the sister what she would do for someone she liked the most. So well did she do this, the sister thought Thérèse really enjoyed her company and considered herself her special friend.

Thérèse already knew of her before she entered, because she had for Thérèse's preparation for her First Communion, given her a pretty chaplet of practices and embroidered the cover of the book Sister Agnès had given her, in which she would write her little acts of self-denial and her practice of the virtues. Described as a peaceable, unassuming nun, but with a rigid personality, she was described by Görres as 'sharp, stupid and conceited'.[10] Thérèse helped her in the sacristy and described her evocatively as a 'potted lily'. It was only after Thérèse's death, and reading her autobiography, that the sister realised she was the one to whom Thérèse had a natural antipathy.

How would she have reacted to this? We do not know, but there are clues: in 1911 she wrote her own reminiscences of Thérèse and the conversations they had together, and they made clear that she understood that Thérèse's friendship with her was genuine, born out of her love for God and which reached down to those most in need. It is often thought that 'charity', which does not have the element of a natural affinity and a human attraction lacks genuine love. But Thérèse shows that a love for someone which looks past a person's character traits, faults and failings, to one created by God and loved by him with an infinite love; one which draws on that love to love that person with God's own love, is far more potent and genuine. That Sister Thérèse of St Augustine seems to have borne no malice towards Thérèse when she discovered the truth seems to imply that she understood this and points to her own generosity of spirit.

True friendship implies the sharing of one's self, and if Thérèse had shown her only a surface relationship it would not have been true. That Thérèse did share herself with Sister Thérèse of St Augustine is demonstrated in conversations we have in 'Last Conversations'. One day, pointing to a medicine that looked delicious the nun remarked, 'I hope you are drinking some good liqueur!' It was in fact very distasteful, and Thérèse replied 'Oh, Sister Thérèse, it's the worst possible thing to drink!'[11]—this, from Thérèse, who normally concealed whatever was distasteful to her.

Later on, Thérèse of St Augustine asked her, with delicious but unconscious irony, 'Tell me, have you had any struggles?' 'Oh yes, I have had some,' Thérèse replied. 'I've had a nature that wasn't easy-going; this wasn't apparent exteriorly, but I know it well, and I can assure you that I wasn't a day without suffering, not a single day.'

'But some think you had none.'

'Ah! the judgments of creatures! Because they don't see, they don't believe!'

'There are some Sisters who believe you will experience the fears of the dying'.

'These haven't come to me as yet. If they should come, I'll bear them; they would be no more than Javel water. What I need is the fire of love.'[12]

Thérèse also allowed her to know about her trial of faith. One day Thérèse confided in her that she no longer believed in eternal life, something that she usually concealed very successfully: 'It seems to me that there is nothing after this mortal life; everything has disappeared, and only love remains.'

'I was strangely surprise to hear of this temptation against faith,' Thérèse of St Augustine said, 'for her soul seemed peaceful and serene as ever; one would have thought that she was flooded by consolation, so easily and naturally did she practice virtue.'

'Oh, if you only knew, if you knew!' replied Thérèse. 'If for five minutes you had to go through the trial I am undergoing! If you only knew!'[13]

An even greater challenge to this divine love in Thérèse came in her relationship with another Sister, Marie of St Joseph. Born Marie Campain in Valkognes, she lost her mother when she was only nine. She entered Carmel 28 April 1881, received the habit 15 October that year and was professed a year later, the same date, 1882. She had such a difficult and sometimes violent temperament that the other sisters avoided her as much as possible, but Thérèse volunteered to help her in the linen room. She described the sister as 'an old clock that had to be rewound every quarter of an hour', and that 'if she had an infirmity such as hers and so defective a spirit, she would despair'.[14] It was not easy, either, for Thérèse to cope with Marie's black moods, because she volunteered to help the sister from March 1986 to May 1897, at a time when she was going through her own dark night of faith and was already ill.

There is a short exchange of notes during the September of 1896[15] when either Thérèse or Marie of St Joseph was on retreat. Thérèse encourages her 'little child' as she calls this nun of thirty eight years old, to recognise that she has a missionary vocation, that by loving she can throw her prayers over the whole world by giving them to Jesus. This was at the time when there was question of sending one of the Martin sisters to Lisieux's foundation in Saigon. Then she calls her 'little brother', who was bearing arms in the combat. Reading between the lines, when Thérèse says that 'he loses his little bit of strength by surrendering his arms to the first corporal [another sister?] who is in his way, and even that he pursues him on the stairs of the barracks', could this be a reference to the sister losing her temper with another sister and even pursuing her down the stairs? She encourages Marie to see herself as a warrior fighting against her weakness.

Thérèse says that the little brother's penance should be to use his musical instrument that evening; a reference to Marie of St Joseph's good singing voice.

In her notes to Marie, Thérèse kept her tone light and encouraging. Marie would suffer periods of deep and dark depression, and Thérèse would encourage her to rest as a little child in Jesus' arms, not taking notice of the dark, resting like Jesus asleep in the boat. It is remarkable, and a testimony to Thérèse's maturity and spiritual development, that a woman nearly twice her age could rely on Thérèse in this way, and that Thérèse's 'spiritual motherhood' could see in this unhappy sister her child. After a night when Marie could not sleep and confided to Thérèse, Thérèse wrote to her:

> How naughty to spend one's night fretting instead of falling asleep on the Heart of Jesus! If the night frightens the little child, if she complains at not seeing Him who is carrying her, let her close her eyes, let her willingly make the sacrifice that is asked of her, and then let her await sleep ... when she keeps herself peaceful

> in this way, the night which she is no longer looking at will be unable to frighten her, and soon calm, if not joy, will be reborn in her little heart.[16]

In her Autobiography Thérèse tells of an occasion[17] which taught her that one cannot make judgments about another, but it also illustrated her delicate consideration for others. While the Community was at recreation some trees arrived and the portress asked for someone to help her bring them in. Mother Subprioress said that Thérèse or Marie of St Joseph could help. Thérèse, thinking that Marie would enjoy going, began undoing her apron slowly to give her the opportunity to volunteer, but Thérèse of St Augustine, sitting on her other side, remarked, 'Ah! I thought as much; you were not going to gain this pearl for your crown, you were going too slowly.'

This little incident also reveals something else. The two sisters whom Thérèse found among the most difficult were sitting on either side of her; Thérèse would sit next to the most unpopular sisters to give them some joy, but it is also probable that sisters sought to sit with Thérèse because they knew they would be welcomed.

Just before Thérèse died, Marie placed a violet on the window sill of the infirmary; the day after her death, Marie smelled the scent of violets and remembered her own gift. This scent of violets and other flowers was a quite frequent phenomenon in the Carmel after Thérèse's death, she who loved flowers so much.

Sadly, Marie left the Community in 1909 when her mental health deteriorated too much for her to remain, after twenty eight years in religion. She was fifty five years old, and found it difficult to adjust to life outside the cloister, spending a wandering existence until her death in 1936, at seventy eight years of age. However, she remained in contact with the Carmel and carried with her the precious notes and also two poems Thérèse had written for her, one, written 'To the Child Jesus' at Christmas 1896, and another, somewhat presciently entitled 'The Eternal Hymn, Sung From Exile'. In 1929 she wrote to Mother Agnès:

> The work of sanctification which my beloved Thérèse began so lovingly in me before she died still continues. And I can say in all sincerity that 'my house is at rest'. And I live now in complete abandonment. As long as I love Jesus, and He and Thérèse are pleased, nothing else matters to me.[18]

With the letter, she returned the notes from Thérèse, apart from one she had given to a sick priest who had begged it from her because of his love for Thérèse.

Although Marie left Carmel, Carmel never left her, and in her wanderings she found the loving abandonment to the good God in whom Thérèse had so encouraged her to trust.

In considering these different sisters and the relations Thérèse had with them, which purified her and inflamed her with the boundless love for God that consumed her, it is easy to lose sight of the pitfalls into which Thérèse could so easily have fallen. A fifteen year old girl who wanted to observe the slightest point of the Carmelite Rule, who admitted that she was not easy-going, could so easily have fallen into the trap of becoming too rigid in her outlook and being judgmental of other sisters not so observant as she was. This was indeed a temptation for her, but Thérèse recognised it and instead sought out the sister's virtues and good intentions. She knew from her own experience how easy it was to misjudge the actions and intentions of others.

It took no little strength of character for her to continue in her own loving and determined observance, her unquestioning obedience to the least command of the very unstable Mother Marie de Gonzague, when the other sisters used common sense in judging whether to obey or not. This was done in such a hidden and unassuming manner that the sisters did not feel themselves under judgment, but simply considered her a pleasant and good little nun, but one who had never really known what it was to have suffered!

Perhaps the last word should be given to Geneviève to describe her effect on the community:

> During the last three years, when I was with her, I noticed that the more clear-sighted among the nuns paid tribute to her exceptional holiness. Sister St Peter, a poor invalid, wanted the charity shown her by Sister Thérèse to be put on record; she even claimed that 'Sister Thérèse would be spoken of later'. Another old nun, since dead, called Sister Marie Emmanuel, said to me: 'This child is so mature and virtuous that were it not for the fact that she is only twenty-two I would like her to be prioress.' Finally, two other old nuns used to go to her secretly for advice. But, all in all, even during these latter years, she continued to lead a rather hidden life, the sublimity of which was better known to God, than those who lived with her.[19]

It was only after her death, with the publication of her autobiography and the 'storm of glory' that followed, that the community found their opinion of Thérèse changing, and they themselves changing in response. Gradually, the sense of God's judgment that needed to be appeased gave way to living in the good God's infinite love. They saw the value of demonstrating their love for God by being faithful in the little things; a community that was so dysfunctional became one that was a true 'school of saints'. The renewed Lisieux Carmel was truly one of Thérèse's greatest miracles, and soon began to attract vocations of great calibre. In death, she became, as it were, the Prioress they didn't have in life.

No account of Thérèse and her sisters could be complete without following her story that little bit further.

Notes

1 Thérèse of Lisieux, *Story of a Soul* (Washington DC: ICS Publications, 1976), translated by J. Clarke OCD, p. 246.

2 Thérèse of Lisieux, *Letters Vol 1.* (Washington DC: ICS Publications, 1982), translated by J. Clarke OCD p. 500.

3 C. O'Mahoney OCD (ed.), *St Therese of Lisieux by Those Who Knew Her* (Dublin: Veritas Publications, 1975), p. 278. See pp. 278–281 for Aimée's testimony.

4 Thérèse of Lisieux, *Letters Vol 1.*, p. 505, note 1.

5 Thérèse of Lisieux, *Story of a Soul, Study Edition* (Washington: ICS Publications, 2005), prepared by M. Foley OCD, translated by J. Clark OCD, p. 370.

6 Therese of Lisieux, *Story of a Soul*, p. 247.

7 P. Descouvemont, *Thérèse of Lisieux and Marie of the Trinity* (New York: St Paul Publications, (Alba House), 1993), p. 31.

8 Thérèse of Lisieux, *Letters Vol 11.* (Washington DC: ICS Publications, 1988), translated by J. Clarke OCD, pp. 1100–1102.

9 Thérèse of Lisieux, *Story of a Soul*, p. 222.

10 I. F. Gorrës, *The Hidden Face* (London: Burns & Oates, 1959), p. 243.

11 P. Martin, (Mother Agnès of Jesus), *St Thérèse of Lisieux, Her Last Conversations* (Washington DC: ICS Publications 1977), translated by J. Clarke OCD, p. 119.

12 *Ibid.*, p. 268.

13 Gorrës, *The Hidden Face,* pp. 260-261.
14 Thérèse of Lisieux, *Story of a Soul, Study Edition,* p. 359.
15 Thérèse of Lisieux, *Letters Vol 11.*, pp. 989-991, 1012–1013.
16 *Ibid.,* p. 1033.
17 Thérèse of Lisieux, *Story of a Soul,* p. 221.
18 Thérèse of Lisieux, *Story of a Soul, Study Edition,* p. 369.
19 O'Mahoney, *Those Who Knew Her*, pp. 154–155.

12

MOTHER ISABEL OF THE SACRED HEART

THÉRÈSE'S DISCIPLE

FOLLOWING THE RUNAWAY success of the publication of *The Story of a Soul* less than three years after her death, Thérèse encouraged not only a host of souls in the world to follow her 'Little Way', but also many young women followed her into the Carmel of Lisieux as well as into Carmels around the world. From being a community, when Thérèse entered it, in which most of the sisters, with a few exceptions, were described as lacking in judgment and good manners, touchy and unkind, her legacy was turning it gently but firmly into a school for saints.

One of these young women was Yvonne Daurelle, who entered the Carmel some six years after Thérèse's death, but who was guided to it by her example and surely through her intercession. Yvonne was born at Epinac, Saône-et-Loire, 29 January 1882, and her early years gave no indication of her future holiness. She had an unsettled childhood, because the family moved several times in the first couple of years of her life, and then, when she was three years old, her mother died. She and two surviving brothers were taken in by their widowed mother's sister, who lived in Mâcon, and who already had two sons of her own; nevertheless, she provided a loving and stable home for the orphans.

Their father left and went to live in Paris, visiting the family every Sunday, until, when Yvonne was five and a half, he went to China. She saw him only three times before she entered Carmel, when he returned to France for a month or two at a time.

Surrounded as she was by four boys, it is unsurprising that she developed into a tomboy, preferring battles, toy soldiers and boxing, rather than dolls. She far preferred the rough and tumble of outdoor play to the prison of the schoolroom, and held her own there only because of her intelligence, which enabled her to keep her grades with the minimum of effort.

This stability was disturbed when her aunt remarried; Yvonne was eleven and became a boarder instead of a day scholar at her school. Like Thérèse, she felt as if she had lost a second mother and had been rejected for a second time, which was a torment to her. She made her First Communion 28 May 1893, but with little devotion and no sense of love for God.

In her teenage years she went through all the teenage angst; she read Lamartine's *Meditations,* and her head was filled with thoughts of ideal love, of the ideal man she might one day meet. She became wrapped up in herself, and as she herself described:

> I had been fairly pleasant to live with until now, for it was natural to me to dislike what was wrong and to be attracted by what was noble. From that time, the more or less commonplace realities of daily life jarred upon me perpetually, and those around me suffered from my bad temper as a result. I repaid kindnesses and attentions with indifference or even with irritability. When old enough to make some return for the devotedness of my adopted mother, I selfishly shut myself up in my room where I

> indulged in foolish dreams and in reading and writing about frivolous subjects.[1]

By now she was living in Paris, but disliked the dust and the noise of the city, preferring the countryside. She had not found her ideal man, although her dreams were becoming less nebulous. Although not pious, her dreaming was gradually maturing into meditation. One early evening, while the sun sank into a glorious sunset, she was thinking of the Trinity when suddenly the world seemed to stop and she was drawn into an apprehension of heaven. She was filled with a longing for the things of heaven, a longing that would never leave her. It was at once a torment, a comfort and a spur, urging her on to reach the true goal of her desires, God himself.

She was now nineteen years old and she soon felt the desire to consecrate herself to God. She read St Teresa of Avila's writings, and reading her words, 'No one can become a saint without undergoing great labours and trials' grasped the wrong end of the stick and, in her own words, became 'a thorough bigot'. She invented severe ways of mortifying herself, spent many hours in prayer, never spoke an unnecessary word and affected an austere manner. Her piety became so exaggerated that, rather than attracting others, she was simply laughed at. St Thérèse eventually came to her aid, and reading her life Yvonne found that her vocation, too, was to be love in the heart of the Church. Then her one aim was to enter the Carmel at Lisieux, but she met with many obstacles. Her spiritual director waited until she was nearly twenty one before contacting the Carmel, and there was great opposition from her family. The wait affected her health and the Carmel felt she would be better suited to the less austere Visitation convent at Caen. This concern was laid to rest when she was examined by M Guérin, who pronounced her perfectly fit. On 13 January 1904, she entered the Lisieux Carmel.

Yvonne, now known as Sister Isabel of the Sacred Heart, had achieved her goal, but her postulancy was far from easy. She, who had longed to enter Carmel, now found that she disliked Carmelite life intensely. Her prayer was dry and, like Thérèse, she found that she was hopeless and slow at the manual work that was part of a postulant's duties. Like Thérèse, her 'angel', Sister Marie-Ange, who introduced her to the life and customs of the community, was also told to correct any faults. When Isabel was asked how she got on with Marie-Ange, only a year older than herself, she replied, 'She annoys me with her lectures; I know what she tells me quite as well as she does.' 'Well, if you know it, why don't you do it?' was the response.

She was so dreamy and forgetful that in the end it was felt that she should leave and try her vocation in an active Order; Isabel was so horrified and upset that the sisters were reassured that, despite everything, she really wanted to persevere. Her period of postulancy was extended beyond the usual six months, but when she finally received the Carmelite habit 15 October 1904, Feast of St Teresa of Avila, her repugnance and fears were completely replaced by a deep peace and joy.

During her Novitiate, like Thérèse, she worked as an assistant in the linen room and refectory, and spent a good deal of her time dusting and sweeping. She had expected great sacrifices and hardships, but was finding that true holiness lay in the small things. Holding her heavy breviary during the Divine Office gave her painful backache, and she found the fasting difficult. A genuine humility began to replace her pretensions to greatness of soul. She was beginning to understand the meaning of Thérèse's 'Little Way'.

Isabel had hoped to make her Profession on 2 February, but this was delayed until 19 March 1906, Feast of St Joseph. Although at first she was disappointed by the delay, that her Profession fell on his feast-day gave her from then on a great devotion to St Joseph. Her Profession retreat was spent in dryness, but on the day she experienced a deep peace.

Isabel's aim in life now was to follow the example of Saint Thérèse, being faithful in the smallest things, denying herself, detaching herself even more from anything that would hinder her union with God. The year 1908 was especially difficult; she had not bothered to tell her superiors about any small health problems she had, and appeared very robust and healthy, following the full austerity of the Rule. She had entered with the assumption that she would be expected to carry on to the end of her strength before saying anything about her health problems, her tiredness or her discomfort. Now, though, her health began to suffer visibly, and during the summer she was given certain relaxations. She began to find her prayer was once again dry, and everything about the life repelled her. This inner turmoil was reflected in her fear of thunderstorms, and the slightest cloud in the sky gave her such anxiety that she had to go back indoors. She should, she said, be made patroness of cowards! This all culminated in a three day period of intense temptation, which she called an onslaught of the demon of pride, saying: 'I would rather have received nothing, rather than receive it from God'. Then, on the third day:

> I entered into the interior of my soul, and seemed to descend into the giddy depths of an abyss

> where I had the impression of being surrounded by limitless space. Then I felt the presence of the Blessed Trinity, realising my own nothingness, which I understood better than ever before, and the knowledge was very sweet. The divine Immensity in which I was plunged and which filled me had the same sweetness. My joy at seeing my own nothingness equalled my indignation at it during those three days.[2]

This experience made a profound impression on her and on her spiritual life, deepening her prayer. She alternated between being immersed in the presence of God and at the same time being acutely aware of her faults and failings, something that is unsurprising: the closer a soul draws towards God, the more acutely do faults and failings appear in his light.

The sense of the divine indwelling made a profound impression on her. She was, she wrote in some notes she made, struck by Thérèse's saying that 'it is true that I shall *see* God in heaven, but I am *with* Him quite as much on earth as I shall be there'. Isabel reflected: 'I thought that this was not a private conviction of our saint, but that she was announcing, with striking lucidity, a mystery of love which perhaps no-one had ever ventured to believe or proclaim before.'[3]

It is quite astonishing that the mystery of the divine indwelling seemed to have been so little known or understood, and was not part of the spirituality of the Lisieux community. It appears that Jesus' words at the Last Supper, when he said that he and his Father would make their dwelling within his disciples, and that the Holy Spirit would also dwell within believers, had not been part of their spirituality. Only two or three years previously, Blessed Elizabeth of the Trinity had died in the Dijon Carmel in 1906, and had lived this mystery to an intense degree. Thérèse had not developed the truth to such a degree but she did understand it; on 31 May 1896, which that year was the Feast of the Holy Trinity, she wrote a poem for Marie of the Trinity, in which she said:

> You, the great God, whom all the heavens adore,
> You live in me, a prisoner night and day.

Sister Thérèse of Saint Augustine, sitting next to her, remarked that she should have said: 'You live *for* me', but Thérèse, with a knowing wink to her novice, replied, 'No, no, I have said it well'.[4]

If this mystery of the Divine Indwelling had been so neglected or, given the immensity of its reality, that the Most Holy Trinity, Father, Son and Spirit, truly dwells in the souls of the baptised, had been hard to express without presumption, then Elizabeth and Isabel could be seen as its apostles, to bring this truth in a more urgent way to those who long for a deeper union with God.

So impressed now was the community with Isabel that, when elections took place in 1909, in which Mother Agnès once more became Prioress, she was elected Subprioress and also appointed as Novice Mistress. The elections were held following the death from tuberculosis of the Prioress and Isabel's former 'angel', Mother Marie-Ange, who had been elected to that post only eighteen months before, despite the fact that she was still in the Novitiate.

By this time there were eight novices in the Novitiate, and Mother Isabel trained them in the way of her beloved Thérèse. With such fervent novices, various issues arose that she had to deal with. Some entered determined to excel in mortification, and she was careful to impress on them that rather than seeking extraneous penances and mortifications, it was better to accept the discomforts of daily life—the heat, the cold, ill-cooked food, uncomfortable clothing, the daily pinpricks and irritations of communal life.

One novice was afraid of Thérèse's saying that 'The more we wish to be given up to love, the more we must be given over to suffering'. Like Thérèse's sister, Marie of the Sacred Heart, the novice was afraid of what God would demand of her. Though if Thérèse had actually thought that God was a sadistic tyrant who enjoyed inflicting pain and suffering, then she would have been contradicting her own awareness of God as a loving and tender Father. Isabel explained that this did not mean that as soon as one made that surrender God would inflict them with suffering; rather, it meant embracing the petty hardships of everyday life, 'to be perfectly faithful and vigilant in the practice of virtue'—this could mean being patient over small inconveniences, adapting oneself to the wishes of others. The fear that God does sometimes ask for deeper suffering can linger, though; after making her Offering to Merciful Love, Thérèse did go through the horrendous sufferings of her last illness, and there is always that call to share in the sufferings of Christ.

To allay that fear, Isabel told them of a certain sister who was afraid of making the Offering in case the spiritual trials she was enduring would be made even worse. However, when she eventually summoned up the courage to do so, she found that she was inundated with unutterable grace and completely delivered from her previous sufferings. If God allows sufferings, the grace of God always accompanies the trial.

It also meant being forgetful of self, as she told another novice who was too concerned about her own sanctity and the beauty of her soul. If she had come to Carmel for this reason, Isabel told her, then she was missing the point, she would not be a true Carmelite, because the Carmelite vocation was to be an apostle for others: holiness, union with God, was sought so that God could act more freely through the Carmelite for the salvation of souls and for their special vocation of praying for priests.

Another time, she reflected that the best way to know whether a novice was truly on the 'Little Way' was how she reacted to her faults and failings. If she was discouraged and downhearted, then she was still a long way off, but if she was truly joyful in recognising her frailty, then she was genuinely humble. This joyfulness was a gift from God, though, and sprang from the inmost recesses of the heart; it could not be feigned.

Shortly after the elections, the Ecclesiastical Tribunal was set up to examine Thérèse's Cause, and although Isabel had never met her personally, she gave testimony to Thérèse's influence on her. She also began the editing of '*The Shower of Roses*', accounts of miracles, answered prayer and healings attributed to Thérèse's intercession. She had been one of those detailed to answer letters that came into the monastery, but at that time the full extent of her literary gifts had not been realised. Now, because testimonies were pouring in daily, new editions had to be brought out yearly, an enormous task which suited Isabel's skills as a writer. The third edition, compiled the year before her death, for example, was 550 pages long, of closely printed text. She was working on the fourth edition even on her death bed. She also compiled the history of the Foundation of the Lisieux monastery and the life of Mother Geneviève.[5]

In 1911, a serious flu epidemic hit the Carmel, but Isabel was almost the only one to escape it. Then, scarcely was the epidemic over than on the Feast of the Ascension she began to suffer from a violent sore throat and headache and bodily pains and the day after had a haemorrhage of the lungs. She was ordered to bed. Her lungs eventually cleared, but it was a foreshadowing of what was to come.

A short time before, she had been given an intimation that her life on earth would be short, so she was disappointed that her time had not yet come. However, she reflected, 'I have been thinking that my impatience to go to heaven was very ungrateful to God… I found comfort in the thought which suddenly occurred to me that I am not kept here to embellish my crown, but to give glory to God and to help the Church.'[6] Her desires, she said, were infinite; she wanted the salvation of souls until the end of time; that priests should reach the heights of sanctity; that souls would be freed to go direct to heaven, that love would reign in all hearts. With this exultant wideness of vision she recognised that even Jesus could not win every heart, but she could unite her prayer to that of Jesus, whose prayer was unceasing, for his desires were hers.

Her health held up until October the following year, when the haemorrhaging began again. Over the winter months she was confined to her cell, only able to attend Mass and receive communion from the oratory. Her health gradually improved again, and she was pleased that she was well enough when her father, aunt and family visited her in the September of 1912. The community also thought her health was improved and voted for her to continue as Sub-Prioress in the elections in November. The sisters noted her simplicity, her gaiety, her gratitude for everything; she was even more affectionate, attentive, and self-sacrificing than ever; hers was a singing soul.

Her good health lasted only until the following October, when the haemorrhage returned. Even then, bedridden, she occupied herself with her writing, giving instruction to her novices, unfailingly smiling and busy. It was a time of great spiritual growth. She meditated long on the Scriptures and disagreed with those who saw the God of the Old Testament as different from that of the Father revealed in the New Testament. To her, the history of the Old Testament was the account of a loving and merciful God guiding an often rebellious and ungrateful people to the joys he willed for them. 'No!' she exclaimed, 'there has never been a law of fear.'

With her love of both Our Lady and St Joseph she meditated long on the life of the Holy Family. 'I have lived for so long in spiritual intimacy with the Holy Family on earth,' she said, 'that I shall feel that I have been with them before when I meet them in heaven.'[7] Reflecting on the Holy Family, she was also brought to a new understanding of the poor.

> It is to meditation on the Holy Family that I owe the love and respect for the poor and for little ones which has taken the place of the aversion and almost disdain I felt for them until I entered Carmel. The lower classes of society seemed to me a race apart from my own. It was not until I lived in the cloister that I truly understood the Evangelical teaching that all men are brothers and equal before God. Before then, I felt a liking for people of refined appearance, and respect

> and sympathy for them, but the reverse for those who looked poor and ignorant.[8]

From then on, she said, she was especially drawn to answer those letters that were ill-written, but that often expressed a profound faith. 'Now I know that the little ones of this world are much nearer the truth.' She could surely recognise, too, God's working in Thérèse's erstwhile novices, Martha and Marie-Madeleine, and other sisters in the community who came from peasant stock, but who were now visibly changed by the saint's influence. As she noted, 'Intellect and intelligence are not at all necessary to advance in "the way". The good God makes *faithful souls* understand the mystery of love'. She possessed both intellect and intelligence, and, like Sister Geneviève, she had learnt how to use them for the glory of God.

Although she was bedridden now, on 9 June 1913, she joined in the community's rejoicing at the official introduction of the Cause of Saint Thérèse, a Cause for which she herself had worked so tirelessly, when the cloisters were hung with garlands and flowers. However, from March the following year her tuberculosis became much more acute. She received the Last Sacraments 11 July and on 29 July entered on her last agony; even then her gratitude and her love for God, expressed in the radiance of her face, were undiminished. On 1 August, in the early hours of the morning, the community were gathered round her bed praying with and for her, but then had to leave her to attend Mass. As the Sanctus bell rang out, her eyes closed and she slipped away to the vision of the God she had loved so intensely, and who had transformed her into holiness in such a short space of time.

On 3 August she was laid to rest between Saint Thérèse and Mother Marie-Ange, or as the community called them, their 'Trio'. Marie-Ange and Isabel of the Sacred Heart were revered in the Lisieux Carmel as true examples of holiness, transformed by the teachings of their Saint. They may have been among the first to follow her into heaven within the community but they were the first of a countless number of souls, inside and outside the cloister, who have followed in her steps ever since.

Mother Agnès of Jesus wrote her obituary notice. She had the sorrow of laying to rest two great Carmelites, Marie-Ange and Isabel, who both died young, and who were shining examples of the 'Little Way' of her beloved sister. During her long years as Prioress, she would see others of her community preceding her into the vision of God, but to all of them she would be, as she had been to Thérèse, the 'little mother'.

Notes

1 Lisieux Carmel, *Mother Isabel of the Sacred Heart, Carmelite Nun of Lisieux 1882-1914* (USA: Kessinger Publishing, 2007), (facsimile), translated by B. Weld-Blundell, p. 13.

2 *Ibid.,* p. 41.

3 *Ibid.,* p. 45.

4 P. Descouvemont, *Thérèse of Lisieux and Marie of the Trinity* (New York: St Paul Publications, (Alba House), 1993), p. 70.

5 See bibliography and Chapter 5, the facsimile published by Kessinger Publications of Mother Genevieve, as well as the facsimile of Mother Isabel of the Sacred Heart.

6 Lisieux Carmel, *Mother Isabel,* p. 64.

7 *Ibid.,* p. 69.

8 *Ibid.,* pp. 71–72.

BIBLIOGRAPHY

Baudouin-Croix, M., *Léonie Martin, A Difficult Life* (Dublin: Veritas Publications, 1993), translated by M. F. Mooney.

Clarke, H. OCarm., *Message of Love, Reflections on the Life of St Therese* (Faversham UK: Carmelite Press, 1976).

Descouvemont, P., *Thérèse of Lisieux and Marie of the Trinity* (New York: St Paul Publications, 1993), translated by Alexandria Plettenberg-Serban.

Gaucher, G., *The Passion of Thérèse of Lisieux* (Victoria: St Paul Publications (Alba House), 1989), translated by Sr A. M. Brennan, ODC.

Gaucher, G., *The Spiritual Journey of St Thérèse of Lisieux* (London: Darton Longman & Todd, 1987), translated by Sr A M Brennan ODC.

Gorrës, I. F., *The Hidden Face* (London: Burns Oates, 1959), translated by R. and C. Winston.

Lisieux Carmel, *Mother Isabel of the Sacred Heart, Carmelite Nun of Lisieux, 1882-1914* (USA: Kessinger Publishing, 2007), translated by B. Weld-Blundell, facsimile edition.

Lisieux Carmel, *The Foundation of the Carmel of Lisieux and its Foundress Reverend Mother Geneviève of St. Teresa (1913)* (USA: Kessinger Publishing, 2007), translated by a Religious of the Society of the Holy Child Jesus, facsimile edition.

Martin, C., (Sister Geneviève of the Holy Face), *My Sister Saint Thérèse* (Rockford Illinois: Tan Books & Publishers, 1959), translated by The Carmelite Sisters of New York.

Martin, P., (Mother Agnès of Jesus), *St Thérèse of Lisieux, Her Last Conversations* (Washington DC: ICS Publications, 1976), translated by J. Clarke OCD.

Martin, Z. and L., *A Call to a Greater Love* (New York: St Paul Publications (Alba House), 2011), translated by A. Connors Hess, edited by Dr F. Renda.

Miller, F. L. STD, *The Trial of Faith of St Thérèse of Lisieux* (New York: St Paul Publications (Alba House), 1998).

Piat, S.-J. OFM, *Céline, Sr Geneviève of the Holy Face* (San Francisco: Ignatius Press, 1997), translated by The Carmelite Sisters of the Eucharist of Colchester, Connecticut.

Redmond, P., *Louis and Zélie Martin* (London: Quiller Press, 1995).

Six, J.-F., *Light of the Night* (London: SCM Press Ltd., 1996), translated by J. Bowden.

Therese of Lisieux, *Letters Vols 1 & 11* (Washington DC: ICS Publications, 1988), translated by J. Clarke OCD.

Therese of Lisieux, *Poems* (London: HarperCollins Publishers, 1997), translated by A. Bancroft.

Therese of Lisieux, *Story of a Soul* (Washington DC: ICS Publications, 1972), translated by J. Clarke OCD.

Thérèse of Lisieux, *Story of a Soul, Study Edition* (Washington DC: ICS Publications, 2005), prepared by M. Foley OCD.

O'Mahoney, C. OCD, (ed.), *St Thérèse of Lisieux By Those Who Knew Her* (Dublin: Veritas Publications, 1975), translated by C. O'Mahoney OCD.

Vinatier, J., *Mère Agnès de Jésus* (Paris: Editions du Cerf, 1993).

Lightning Source UK Ltd.
Milton Keynes UK
UKOW04f2340131214

243058UK00002B/4/P

9 780852 44846